WILL THE REAL YOU PLEASE STAND UP

33 Ways to Reinvent Yourself

Bee Soars

WILL THE REAL YOU PLEASE STAND UP: 33 WAYS TO REINVENT YOURSELF
www.willtherealyou.com

Copyright © 2021 BEE SOARS

ISBN: 978-1-77277-401-6

All rights reserved. No portion of this book may be reproduced mechanically, electronically, or by any other means, including photocopying, without permission of the publisher or author except in the case of brief quotations embodied in critical articles and reviews. It is illegal to copy this book, post it to a website, or distribute it by any other means without permission from the publisher or author.

Limits of Liability and Disclaimer of Warranty
The author and publisher shall not be liable for your misuse of the enclosed material. This book is strictly for informational and educational purposes only.

Warning – Disclaimer
The purpose of this book is to educate and entertain. The author and/or publisher do not guarantee that anyone following these techniques, suggestions, tips, ideas, or strategies will become successful. The author and/or publisher shall have neither liability nor responsibility to anyone with respect to any loss or damage caused, or alleged to be caused, directly or indirectly by the information contained in this book.

Medical Disclaimer
The medical or health information in this book is provided as an information resource only, and is not to be used or relied on for any diagnostic or treatment purposes. This information is not intended to be patient education, does not create any patient-physician relationship, and should not be used as a substitute for professional diagnosis and treatment.

Publisher
10-10-10 Publishing
Markham, ON
Canada

Printed in Canada and the United States of America

Table of Contents

Foreword ix
Acknowledgements xi

Chapter 1: Reverse Creation 1
The Master Key to Unlimited Possibilities 5
Connecting the Dots 7
Life Tabs 8
The Magic Power of Your Image 11
Contract with Yourself 13

Chapter 2: How to Discover Who You Are
and Then Behave Like It 15
You Are a Superhero 19
How to Develop Your Superpowers 24
Your Purpose and Why You Are Here 25
Wishes Your Heart Makes 28

Chapter 3: I Am My Goal 31
Speaking Your Desires into Reality 35
Creating Your Own Incantations 36
Aligned Magic 40
The Power of Intention 42
Can You See It? 44
The Stories You Tell Yourself 48
Mission Statement 51

Chapter 4: #CATCHUPTOHER 53
Pixie, the Adorable Active Little One 57
Rebella, the Beautiful Rebellious Girl 59
Enchantress, the Charming Romantic Healer 62
Journaling 63

Chapter 5: Ditch the Crabs 65
Words You Speak...69
The Lies You Tell Yourself...72
Fears Are Prayers for What You Don't Want....................................77
Get Comfortable Feeling Uncomfortable 80
Clean up Your Clutter 81
Energy Vampires..83
Creating a Personal Inventory 84
Letting Go of Resentment 85

Chapter 6: When You Forget Who You Are 89
Triggers Are Your Guides 93
Stop Reacting, Start Living...94
Don't Think; Feel 96
Multiple Layers of Reality 100

Chapter 7: Money Has Ears and It Hears When You Call 103
Find Your Own Version of Happiness 107
Remember: No Deposit, No Return 108
Be Grateful for Your Bills 113
Money Affirmations 114

Chapter 8: Receiving Is the Twin Sister of Asking......................117
Be Open to Receive 121

Chapter 9: Elle et Lui 125
Masculine and Feminine Energies..129
Are You Using Too Much Masculine Energy? 132

Chapter 10: SELF **133**
What is Self? 137
Self-Discovery – Powerful Questions to Help You Know Yourself ... 139

Chapter 11: When You Meet You **141**
Gratitude 149
Secrets of Life 149
Celebration 151

About the Author 157

I dedicate this book to you—I knew you would come.

Foreword

This book made its way into your hands for a reason. Maybe a friend suggested you buy it, maybe you got it as a gift, or maybe something else led you to it. When you are ready, the book you need finds you.

Will the Real You Please Stand Up will show you how you are the point of attraction to everything you desire in life. You will shift in ways you never even imagined possible. Your life will have more flow and you probably won't even remember what being stuck felt like. If you do, you will have all the tools to get yourself back on track. This book will help you gain access to the part of you that has been hiding. It will open you up.

Bee Soars has a special way of reaching out. It's like her words have the frequency of love. You will feel as if she is always there holding your hand while you recreate yourself. You will feel loved, loveable and able to love again after reading this book. Bee will show you many ways to create a beautiful life for yourself.

Bee has crafted all the steps for you to take in a way that is easy to understand and apply. You will notice shifts as you go on your journey of self-discovery and mastery.

Make sure you read everything, and do everything as if your life depended on it, because it does. These are the tools you have been looking for. Bee will help you awaken that power inside of you and live your life with purpose.

Raymond Aaron
New York Times Bestselling Author

Acknowledgements

I am thankful for all the beautiful people that showed up in my life and have helped me celebrate all the happy moments, or showed up when I needed them the most.

I would like to thank all the mentors, friends, and coaches that I have met along the way and who have transformed my life. Thank you for helping me find my calling and be unafraid to become the person I showed up in this life to be.

I want to thank Nicole Hyatt for her friendship throughout the years, and for all the business and life advice she gave me while having coffee at her kitchen table.

I would like to thank Raymond Aaron for his wisdom, teachings, and guidance throughout the writing of my book, and for believing in me and what I am here to do in the world.

I want to thank Sonny and Carlos. Both of you, without even realizing it, made a huge difference in my life when I was going through the darkest time in my life.

I want to thank Warren Ryan for showing up on my Facebook newsfeed with a "love yourself" challenge, where I got to step out of my comfort zone and offer free hugs to strangers on the street.

I would like to thank Suzanna and Richard for teaching me to show up and be seen as me, and not as the person I think others want me to be.

Will the Real You Please Stand Up

I am thankful for John-Erik, for mentoring me about social media and, most importantly, for being human and loving on people while being active online.

Thanks to all my clients for showing up with love and trust, and for helping me to adapt the tools in this book to make it easy for my reader to use. It has been an amazing experience to watch you transform.

I am so grateful for my fiancé, for always supporting me and all my crazy ideas, pushing me to go after my dreams, and helping me create a better life for my boys.

I would like to thank my amazing parents for always cheering for me, supporting all my decisions, and being a great example of unconditional love, which I hope I am able to pass on to my boys just the way I received it. You are two role models that I am extremely proud to call my parents. Thanks for giving me a perfect childhood and memories. Dad, your yellow Porsche is on its way.

Finally, I want to thank my boys: Gabe, Nick, and Tchuka. You are the reason I do everything I do and never give up. I have been blessed with the opportunity to experience life with you. Being your mom is the best gift I have ever received. I am super proud of the young men you are.

Chapter 1

Reverse Creation

"Every day, you reinvent yourself. You are always in motion. But you decide every day: forward or backward."
— James Altucher

The Master Key to Unlimited Possibilities

I have spent the last 10 years of my life trying to find answers. The more I learned, the things I already knew started to make more sense. I had acquired so much knowledge, yet it didn't really seem like I was getting anywhere. Nothing was changing.

I realized I had to find a way to start implementing what I learned intentionally, and the answer I got was to write this book. When I started to write it, the intention was to create my own personal manual: a guide with tools using the techniques that have worked for me in the past so that I could replicate the process to achieve similar results over and over again in all areas of my life.

I knew that the tools I am about to share with you worked. They have worked for me, as well as for my coaching clients. It's a lot easier to teach and share than it is to do it yourself. I noticed that I was so focused on my clients that I wasn't really following my own guidance. I knew that in order to really do that, I had to go first. What better way to show others than by leading by example? So I did.

As I started to write this book, my life started to change again. Friends and family started to approach me, asking me what I was doing. They were curious to know how I was changing my life, at what for them seemed like an incredible speed. Seeing that it had worked for me, and for others around me, I decided that I had to share it with as many people as I could.

Will the Real You Please Stand Up

Since I had decided that I would lead first, I made the decision that before this book got to your hands, I would apply all the tools in my life as I wrote each step. I am so glad that I did it. I had no doubts, and by doing it, life transformed again.

Now, listen up, buttercup: I want to make sure you know and understand that whatever you believe your reality to be, and accept that reality as your truth, it will be.

If you think you cannot change your reality, and accept that as that, it will be just that.

However, if you decide that you can choose your reality and reinvent yourself as often as you want to, you will find opportunities and people to help you along the way. Consider me one of those people. I got you, babe!

There is a reason you picked up this book—you know that, right?

Close your eyes; hold the book with both hands. Can you feel it? You are now holding the master key to unlimited possibilities.

It's not so much about what you will read,
but it is everything about what you will find.

Connecting the Dots

I remember listening to an amazing speech given by Steve Jobs in 2005. It was probably one of the most important speeches I had ever heard.

"You can't connect the dots looking forward; you can only connect them looking backwards. So you have to trust that the dots will somehow connect in your future. You have to trust in something—your gut, destiny, life, karma, whatever. This approach has never let me down; it has made all the difference in my life."
– Steve Jobs

When I first heard this quote, I had a different understanding, and as my life started to change, the way I understood those words changed too.

I thought the meaning behind it was that you could try to plan life knowing that unpredictable things would come your way, and even without understanding, you would just have to know that it would all make sense in the end. Simple.

A few years later, I heard the same quote again, but this time was so different. I wasn't the same person either, which probably contributed to the different perspective I had. You need to understand that as you grow, the way you see things change, so it's important to see what beliefs and ideas you are holding onto that no longer serve you, and create new ones.

If you can't connect the dots looking forward, but only backwards, the only way to understand it would be to trust the process and wait for it, right?

What if, instead, you started at the end, and by connecting the dots backwards, you reverse created your ideal life?

Most people know exactly what they don't want; they focus most of their time on the unwanted, and only have a vague idea of what they want.

When you start from the end, you stop trying to figure out who society and others want you to be, and you get to decide who you want to be instead.

Once you decide and can visualize that scenario in your mind, magic will start to happen. Your subconscious will start to show you things that match your visual description, and it will help you notice opportunities coming your way.

Think of this book as a map. This map will help you understand how you work, what makes you sing, what drives you, and what you are here to do; and most importantly, it will guide you to your true self—the real you.

Life Tabs

I think one of the best feelings I ever experienced was when I felt things happening not by chance but intentionally. I was writing a new script, and it was working. I want you to feel it too, and when you do trust me, you will experience life in a new way, and you will fall in love with yourself again.

Start by choosing who you want to be; and since everything is connected, you need to look at the overall picture as a whole. Every area of your life impacts another. For the best ongoing results, you need to create a new script that includes every area. Everything needs to be in harmony. There are lots of sections, and everyone is different, but here is a list of areas you might want to include when reverse creating your life. I call them life tabs.

My Life Tabs

- Family/Inner Circle
- Finances/Cash Flow/Wealth
- Love
- Home Environment
- Career/Work/What I Can Offer
- Spiritual/Personal Growth
- Body
- Health/Nutrition
- Self-Esteem
- Self-Care
- Social Life
- Creativity/Expression
- Contribution/How I Can Serve
- Self
- Bucket List

Create your own life tabs. On your list, circle the ones you know you want to work on immediately. Try not to leave anything out; in order to have balance, they all need to be working together in alignment. Once your list is created, envision what would be ideal for each of them, and just write everything down. Let it come to you. There is no right or wrong; just write everything that comes to your mind.

Here is an example of what my FAMILY tab looks like:

- Unconditional love
- Strong commitment to each other
- Appreciation for one another

Will the Real You Please Stand Up

- Affection
- Prioritize time together
- Manage stress and crisis effectively
- Think of ways to pull together rather than fall apart
- Encourage emotions
- Acceptance of individual uniqueness
- Fun times
- Positive and respectful communication
- Healthy lifestyle
- Understand that mistakes and misunderstandings are part of life
- Forgiveness
- Attempt to make a family member feel special daily
- Ask questions; don't judge
- Give full attention when they are speaking
- Laugh together
- Ask often what they like about our family and what they don't
- Create memories
- Apologize
- Think before speaking
- Say "I love you" every day, even if it's through a text message
- Hugs
- Always wish them good night
- We are all the same; we learn together
- Cause smiles

These are the things that are important to me. Your family can become stronger by focusing on areas you want to improve. Try not to be too vague. Having a strong family is a nice goal, but if you get more specific, it will be easier to know *how* to have a strong family. Remember, there is no right or wrong. What is important for me might be totally different for you.

Think of the things you love about each area, and the things you want to love. Leave out anything that does not make you smile when you think about it. The list should only include what you want to keep or create.

Everything you want already exists, and it's just waiting for you. This book will show you how to claim what is already yours.

You will learn how to apply simple but powerful techniques, step by step, and notice changes as you go. It gets to be that easy.

Remember, you are not connecting the dots; you are tracing the already connected dots. It does not have to be complicated!

These tools can work for everyone; there are no exceptions—as long as you believe, they can work.

Believe you can do it, or it will not work.

The Magic Power of Your Image

Who are you really?

Before you can become **IT,** you have to know what **IT** is. Creating your self-image is where it all starts. The way you see yourself has the power to transform your world.

By now you have an idea of people you admire, from TV shows, magazines, or people you actually know. You know what you like about them and what you don't, but this is not about them; it's about you. It's about creating the image you have of yourself.

When I was in my early teens, I used to collect pictures from magazines that I liked, and I hung them all over my bedroom wall. I had pictures of outfits, make-up, and hairstyles; and sometimes it was about the attitude the person had—how she carried herself. The idea was that I would get inspired by those pictures and, little by little, I would shift my identity, becoming like the people in the pictures.

Will the Real You Please Stand Up

Now it's time to apply those qualities and attributes you admire, to your self-image. Please don't do this exercise focusing on what other people would like. This is about you and only you.

Take a few minutes to relax. Breathe in; breathe out.

Imagine that you are looking through a magazine, and you found a picture you like.

Now imagine that it's a picture of you—The REAL YOU! Pay attention to all the details. Colors! Attitude! Feel the energy! The more details you imagine, the more real it gets!

See yourself being that! It is you! It's an entire article about you! Your mini biography—all the steps you took to be who you are today! Now feel the feeling of how many other lives you are impacting by sharing your story about becoming you, the real you.

There is a reason why you have those desires. Some say that in a different reality, you are living that exact life, and that is why you feel connected to it. Now that's a different topic for another time.

One thing I am sure of is that you wouldn't have those desires if you weren't able to achieve them. Your desires are the attraction energy pulling you to the things that are made for you. They are reminders of who you are; glimpses of all the possibilities of the life you are intended to have.

Now see yourself living that life. Make this a habit, and practice it with intention. Do it for at least 33 days. It takes anywhere from between 21 days and 41 days to create a new habit, but I find that there is something magical about doing it 33 times. All you need is a few minutes a day. If you prefer, tell yourself your story before you go to bed. See yourself the way you saw in the magazine. Add sounds and feelings; use all senses.

www.willtherealyou.com

Contract with Yourself

If you want to succeed, you have to commit yourself to do it. I will help you along the way, but only you have the power to create a new self. It's normal that moments of self-doubt will show up. When they do, it's what you do that will make a difference.

If you give up and go back to doing what you have been doing, you will just keep being your old self. Don't get confused; stay focused. Have the confidence to trust yourself.

On the next page, or on a separate piece of paper, create a contract to help you keep going when self-doubt creeps in. Tonight, before you go to sleep, work on it. Write down your why: the reason *why* you are committing yourself to becoming the best version of yourself. What will you no longer tolerate?

Write it as if you were writing a letter to yourself from the future, when you are about to give up but your future self knows what you are just about to become. What can she tell you that will prevent you from giving up? Make it powerful, as if your life depended on it. Don't forget to sign it. Keep this contract in an envelope in your drawer. If you ever feel like giving up, open it!

Will the Real You Please Stand Up

Chapter 2

How to Discover Who You Are and Then Behave Like It

"We can only be what we give ourselves the power to be."
– Native American Proverb

You Are a Superhero

If I say the word *superpower*, what is the first thing that comes to your mind? Wonder Woman, Batgirl, Storm, Enchantress? Most people will think of superhero characters from movies they have seen, discarding the possibility that they too have superpowers. The truth is that we all do.

You might be thinking that I am talking gibberish and that you have no superpowers, but let me break it to you, Hun: You do, and I am going to help you discover and use them.

Your powers are unique, and just like no human being can have the same fingerprints, no one will have the same powers that you do. Sometimes it takes someone else seeing in you what you can't see for yourself first, but that's not the fastest way.

We all have unique abilities within ourselves. You might not have noticed them before, or something happened in your life that kept them dormant, or you might have been told not to act or feel a certain way. They might be hidden, but I will share a little secret I have discovered over the years.

Please promise me that you won't wait until you have developed them to start using your powers. If you wait to be ready to start using them, you will be starting too late.

Will the Real You Please Stand Up

Millions of people spend their whole lives searching, and most of them never end up finding them, because they are looking for something outside, not realizing that they're already within.

Superpowers are not the skills you are good at because you practiced them over time. They are way more than that.

Now that you understand that you too have something in you that makes you unique, you are probably wondering what that power is, or maybe even thinking that you don't have it. I can assure you that we all do, and I will tell you how to find it.

Your superpower is that thing you think you lack, and admire in others.

Crazy, right? I know... but if you think about it, it totally makes sense. You would never have noticed it in others if you didn't have it within you. You only noticed it because you identified yourself with it.

What we see in others is a reflection of ourselves. Every person you meet is like a mirror; they bring within them something you need to either heal or remember.

We get to learn more about ourselves when we interact with others. You find a little bit of yourself in everyone you meet, especially those that you admire.

Someone's personality traits may trigger a negative emotion in you. This usually means that something within you is coming up to be healed and released. It could appear as an experience that keeps repeating itself, which in that case is happening because, instead of dealing with it, you are ignoring it and pretending it doesn't exist.

This triggered feeling could come up as something you dislike in another person, and avoiding that person will just keep bringing more people with the same things you dislike into your life. I will tell you more about triggers and what they actually are, in Chapter 6.

This could be the result of having something similar in yourself that you dislike, or which causes the same emotion in others. People are showing you who you are, and providing the opportunity to love yourself by accepting it or working on it.

This is also the case with your hidden superpowers. The qualities you admire in others are also within yourself. The reason that you are noticing them is for you to remember who you are, develop those powers, and fall in love with the real you.

Look around you—what do you see in others? Obviously, you should be looking for the things you love in people, since those are the powers you want to develop. Let's not focus on the negative traits right now, as those are not what we are looking to amplify. You need to work on developing your powers. Once you figure it out and master it, you will live a life that the average person doesn't even know exists.

Your superpower is a tool to be used to manifest the life you desire— even better, to live on purpose with a purpose.

There are some other ways you can find clues to help you discover what powers you have. I have included an exercise at the end of the chapter to help you.

We definitely need more superheroes in this world, and there is a superhero version of you out there waiting to be found.

Embrace your powers. We all have them. Seeing things you admire in others is not only a reflection but a reminder that you are all born with a special gift. No one else can express it the way you can. It's like a recipe that a lot of people might cook, but each person adds their own secret ingredients.

Will the Real You Please Stand Up

I am going to help you awaken your dormant power. I hope you are as excited as I am.

As kids, your powers show up but, like most people, you forget about them as you start to grow up. Most likely, you had people tell you to be like everyone else and do what everyone else is doing. Some even made you believe that you were not good enough. That's how limiting beliefs are created and dreams are crashed.

That's okay; you can still go back to childhood and resuscitate those dreams. Think back to when you were a kid. Start by recalling events, memories, and people. Think of all the details you can remember.

I was born in Brazil, and my first language is Portuguese. As a kid, I remember that I always wanted to be a teacher. My friend, Luiza, and I used to pretend that we were teachers, and we taught our students in English. Back then, I had no knowledge of English; it was just pretend. In our play, we spoke English fluently; even though to others, we were speaking gibberish. We even created songs in that made-up English language.

Today, I know that my power is in my voice. I am here to guide and show others many possible directions and ways to create a beautiful abundant world. Were my make-believe plays clues? Of course they were. When I was 15, my parents decided to move our family to Canada, and now I am an intuitive coach, sharing my tools and knowledge with my clients, in English, all over the world.

After all the years of telling myself lies, I was under the belief that I lacked confidence and clarity. I thought I was too shy and, like most people, subconsciously not enough.

The tools that I am sharing with you in this book work, and I have applied them in my life over and over, and continuously do so. I did the work. I wanted to make sure these tools work and that it wasn't just a fluke.

When I started to write this book, I went to spend a week with my parents. We spent the entire week remembering my childhood and looking through old pictures. I wanted to know what else I enjoyed doing as the "little me."

I had completely forgotten about being in a school play, and even though I didn't have too many lines, I was one of the characters that didn't leave the stage. I was with other characters, narrating the story while it happened, in the background. The "little me" wasn't shy at all.

Another time, when I was in grade 5, I participated in a writing contest, competing against all the students in the school, and I won third place. It was a little poem about life and nature. I had to read it in front of all the students, their families, and teachers. It was a little scary, but I did it anyway. Without fear, there can be no courage, right?

If you can't remember what the "little you" liked to do, I recommend that you speak to your parents, family, and old friends. They can probably help you to bring back some memories. If you have the opportunity to go back where you grew up, take a walk through your old neighborhood.

You can even search for places and things on the internet if you can't go back, or if the neighborhood has gone through major changes. It will probably help you awaken lost feelings and thoughts that have been sleeping in your subconscious. I had so much fun re-experiencing childhood memories and going down memory lane. I felt like I was that same kid all over again.

How about you?

Will the Real You Please Stand Up

What was your favorite thing to do as a child?

What did you do the most? Who were you when you played pretend?

Everything that has happened in your life up to now, especially in your childhood, are major clues to your magic.

How to Develop Your Superpowers

Think about it. Superheroes are always showing us how to lead and help improve the lives of others around us. Ask yourself how you can do the same, and start there.

There is a multiplier effect when what you love to do helps others around you. This could be as little as saving the planet, or as big as being a stay-at-home mom raising her family. If you are a mom, have a mom, or know a mom, you will understand how big of a job that is.

You now have a couple of the tools I use with my coaching clients to help them identify their powers. One is to go down memory lane, and the other is to pay attention to the things you admire in other people. I will share an exercise that I have my clients do. This exercise will help you get more clarity.

On a blank sheet of paper, make a list of at least 5 people you admire. Go ahead and grab it now. Don't just keep reading, telling yourself that you will do it later. It won't be the same. Take a few minutes to think about these people. You don't have to actually know them. They could be actors from a movie, people you have seen walk by you, friends, someone that caught your attention—basically anyone.

For each one of them, start writing down all the things you noticed and loved; things that made you think to yourself how you wished you had these same things.

Was it the way they walked? Talked? How did they interact with people? Include all the details.

The things you noticed are the key elements of your superpowers, and with time you can perfect them.

Finding your superpowers will help you discover the path to the real you, which may lead to something even bigger...your beautiful purpose.

After reading this book, you will understand yourself in ways you never imagined before. You will find missing pieces of your puzzle.

Your Purpose and Why You Are Here

Your superpowers are connected with your purpose. Purpose is not what you do but who you are.

The search for your purpose in life will take you down a path of reconnecting with your childhood memories and dreams.

Everything that has happened in your life up to this point were clues; clues to guide you to your purpose, the reason you are here.

All your experiences are like hints—pieces of a puzzle—to guide you to remember who you are, and help others see in you who they are. **Aww, I love this!**

One of the things I get asked the most by my clients is how they can find their purpose. This has to be one of my favorite topics. Have you ever asked yourself that question? Why are you here?

A few people grow up knowing what it is; others discover it over time, and some never find it.

Start by asking yourself questions about what makes you happy and what doesn't. Life is full of questions, and they lead you to the answers, which are your clues of paths to follow. Changing your blueprint is the best way to change what is not working, and to find meaning in life.

If you are depressed, sad, and anxious, it is most likely because there is a part of your life that is not matching what you believe it should be. I am not talking about a setback when something bad happens and leaves you feeling sad.

I am talking about a crisis coming from deep within, from your soul. When all emotions, like depression, sadness, and despair, are present, but this crisis was not caused by an outer issue, it has a bigger purpose, just like you do.

This type of crisis usually happens when you are not being your real self, and it is trying to lead you to all the possibilities. It breaks you down so you can put yourself back together again.

I remember having a conversation with an old friend, who at the time was playing for the Raptors, one of the teams in the NBA. I asked him what made him want to play basketball besides being over 7 feet tall. His answer was magical. He said he grew up hating how tall and different he was compared to his friends. He lacked confidence and self-esteem, until the day he was introduced to basketball for the first time. His exact words were, "It was the day I understood why God made me so tall."

Stop doing all the empty "doings" that fill up your day, and start doing and being what actually matters. Do the things that light that spark you have inside of you.

What can you now do with your time that will give you that happy feeling?

What can you now do with your time that will make someone else smile?

Don't think; feel it! What's the first answer that comes to you before your mind takes over and starts giving you all the reasons you shouldn't do what you are here to do?

Don't settle for anything less than what you intend to be, have, and do. Life makes ways when you decide to make your move. You choose.

Don't get me wrong; I am not saying that it will always be easy. Life will definitely test you to see if what you say you really want is actually true. This is where most people fail—they settle for what shows up, not realizing that what they wanted was just around the corner. I have seen it happen with jobs, relationships—you name it. Don't let it happen to you too.

Get your journal out. Actually, you should just keep it with you at all times when reading this book. It will make it easy for you to start implementing these techniques right away.

I shared this book with a few of my clients. They spent a few days working on the new tools they learned, and then came back to tell me how things started to change almost immediately.

Play the "what if" game and let your heart take you on a journey of self-discovery.

What if you could not fail; what would you choose to do?

What if you had everything you wanted; how would you spend most of your days?

What if money was not an issue; what would you be doing right now?

Would you start a business?

Would you spend more time with friends and loved ones?

What would you do if you could just be you?

Wishes Your Heart Makes

If you had no memory, whom would you choose to be? What role would you play in this lifetime?

Most people know what they don't want, but they never stop to think about what they actually desire in life.

If you go out on the street and start asking random people if they know what they want out of life, most people won't be able to answer. They will start to tell you all the things they don't want in their lives but don't really know the things they want to have, do, or be.

They program their subconscious, giving it directions, but in a negative way. As a result, they end up getting more of those things, because those are the things they spent most of their time thinking about.

It's time you develop a plan. Listen to your desires. Let them guide you to the real you. You wouldn't have these desires if you didn't have the means to achieve them. Your desires are wishes your heart makes.

Envision how you want your life to be, and make plans as if all the things you want already exist.

How would the person you would like to become do the things you are about to do?

Start by developing the muscles of your mind. For the next 33 days, set aside some time for you to exercise your mind.

Start with a blank sheet of paper and, at the top, write down your name, followed by a list of qualities, skills, and traits you want to develop.

For the next 20 minutes or so, start writing down things you can do to become that version of yourself. Don't think too much; just write them down as they come, even if they seem crazy.

Every idea will trigger another idea. Some ideas will be so good, while others will be useless, but you will be creating a new habit and, with time, new ideas will start flowing to you.

I suggest carrying a little notebook with you at all times as you will start to notice ideas showing up out of the blue. You need to take those inspirations seriously. They are guiding you to achieve your desires and goals, and you should act on them immediately. A single idea could be all it takes.

You need to make sure your goals are what you want, not what others want or what you think you should want. If your goals are not exciting enough to get you out of bed, maybe they are not for you. You will have an idea by the way you feel when you think about them.

If you keep on trying and committing yourself to the same goals over and over, and nothing is happening, there is a chance that your beliefs are limiting you, or they are someone else's goals that you told yourself were yours.

I remember reading somewhere about how Michael Jackson woke up one day around 3 a.m., thinking about butterflies, and he immediately called his producer, waking him up and saying that they needed to start working on the next song, and he kept saying butterflies.

Will the Real You Please Stand Up

His producer told him that they would start working on it in the morning, but Michael insisted that they start immediately: "We need to act quick, cause if we don't, Prince will." The song was his last single and was top 14 on the Billboard Hot 100 singles, in 2002.

Life whispers in your ear, but sometimes you are so busy trying to prove and impress others that you don't hear the calling.

It doesn't matter what your goal is. Whether it's to be the next best version of yourself, to buy a new car, have multiple streams of income, or to be the best mom you can be, just decide what your goal is, and imagine what you would be like as that person.

Remember, you already have the resources and the potential to achieve whatever you want, inside yourself. The most important thing you need to do at this point is to decide what it is that you want.

Start seeing yourself as the woman that is already living the life you intend to have. Focus on the feeling; imagine how you will feel when you have achieved your desires, and feel that feeling now.

What would have had to happen for you to achieve your desires? What steps would you have had to take to get there, for you to become her? Those steps should definitely be on the list you are creating.

Don't get caught up on the "how." You don't need to know how right now; trust that you will be guided to your goal, and your "how" will show up. Focus on "what," not on "how."

Chapter 3

I Am My Goal

"What you get by achieving your goals is not as important as what you become by achieving your goal."
– Zig Ziglar

www.willtherealyou.com

Speaking Your Desires into Reality

As you can see, every tool and topic in this book go together. It's my recommendation that you apply all of them to all areas of your life. You don't have to do them all at once. Decide how often you are willing to do the work, and stick to it.

I offer a program, #catchuptoher, where we work together on each step; and the most results I have seen came from the ones that stayed committed and did the work. It might take time and lots of patience, but once you understand how you work inside out, life will transform.

Your desires will come to you as fast as you can receive them. When you think and decide what you want, your desires will come to you. But it's only when you take action that you will receive them.

As you read this book and use the tools it provides you, you are reprogramming your mind. By repeating something over and over, you get things stuck in your mind, and that's what affirmations do for you. However, I noticed that the only affirmations that were working for me were the ones I was emotionally attached to. I played around with them and noticed that affirmations alone don't work.

Have you been using affirmations and seeing no results?

That's because affirmations are only one of the ingredients. You need to create your own incantations instead. Incantations are supercharged affirmations—like an upgraded version. You need to add emotions and reactions to it. How would you feel if what you are saying was already in your reality? Don't just say it out loud; SCREAM IT!

Your mind will start to believe in it, and if you convince yourself that this is going to transform your life, it will.

One of the reasons I love incantations is that you can do them as many times or as few times as you want, throughout your day. Create a time dedicated to do them. I have an alarm set twice a day to remind me to do them when I am having a busy day. I commit them to memory and think and speak them whenever I am able to, such as when I am driving or even getting things done around the house. Combining it with visualization will make them even more powerful.

Use this time to visualize your desires and speak your incantations as if they are already done. Play with it. Keep in mind your end goal, and make sure it is in alignment with your beliefs.

Don't use them if you don't believe what you want is possible. Your subconscious accepts the thoughts with the strongest emotion. If you have doubts and contradicting thoughts to your desires, you will create resistance every time you say it.

If your beliefs prevent you from trusting and believing your words, you will need to get rid of the clutter in your mind first, which is limiting you.

Creating Your Own Incantations

Make them short and sweet; it will be easier for you to memorize them. If you can repeat them 3–5 times in a row without struggling, they are perfect.

Use present tense; your subconscious doesn't know the difference. Adding the word "now," or "right now," will make it even more powerful.

You can also create a few using "I remember when," as if you were your future self, remembering life before achieving your ideal life. Again, tricking your subconscious mind...

Create a mix of statements: things that haven't happened yet, and things that have happened. It will help you trust and believe.

"I AM" statements are super powerful; whatever follows the "I AM," programs your mind. They are like commands for your subconscious.

Don't use negative words, like don't, can't, won't, etc. You want to feel positive when you say them. They need to be focused on what you want, and not on the things you don't want.

Make it personal; you can use others as inspiration, but add your own touch to it. By creating it yourself, you are visualizing your end goal; and every time you say it, the same images and feelings will be triggered automatically.

Don't forget to include emotions—you need to feel it as you speak it. Use your body and your voice.

Include other people when creating your incantations. Knowing what is wanted creates energy to manifest, but wishing abundance for others multiplies the effect. My favorite one is: **What I want for myself, I want for everybody else.**

I noticed with my clients that when they were using the same ones for too long, they make you lose focus, and they stop carrying the same energy. I recommend changing them every week or two. Five lines are the ideal.

Some superheroes use magic words to activate their powers. Your words are powerful and have the ability to influence your own reality. If they are not working, it is because you are not convincing enough.

There is a powerful magic about writing them down and not just creating them in your head.

Use the space on the next page to start creating your own incantations. I have included my favorite ones to give you an idea. Make sure yours are related to the things you want and desire. Writing them on sticky notes all over the house is a fantastic way to not forget them.

- **Everything I say is intentional and on purpose.**
- **Everything is always working out for me.**
- I am so happy I can't stop smiling.
- I have money to share and spare.
- I am a woman that leads by example.
- I have a healthy and fit body.
- **Every time I spend money, money comes back to me multiplied.**
- I am always at the right place at the right time.
- I see beauty in everything, everywhere I go and no matter whom I am with.
- I am a mother that positively supports my children in living their lives with ease, elegance, and joy as much as possible.
- I now make money doing what I love.
- I am a woman with a voice.
- I am inviting abundance into my life right now.
- I am so happy and grateful that I pay my bills in full and on time.
- I am new every morning.
- I am impeccable with my words.
- I speak my desires into existence.
- I am balanced in speaking and listening.
- I am a woman who is comfortable speaking my mind.

- I feel safe to express myself.
- I am young, strong, and cannot grow old.
- I am seen.
- I am a woman with a purpose.
- I accept myself, the goddess that I am.
- I do not want or hope; I intend.
- My home is safe and secure.
- I am always safe.
- I communicate confidently and with ease.
- When I speak, my words have power.
- I am a powerful creator.
- I am comfortable speaking my mind.
- Temporary life incidents have no power over me.
- My inner power is indestructible.

Aligned Magic

Every moment, every situation provides a new choice. Life is always in action, action is always creating abundance, and you create your life by making choices. There has to exist a balance between taking action and knowing when to let it flow.

What are you doing to choose your life?

Don't lose yourself in daily chores and empty doings. Think of some actions that are aligned with your goals.

List the actions that are not aligned with your goals, and stop doing them.

Move only if it feels good.

Act on ideas immediately if it feels right, even if it makes no sense.

Make fewer decisions.

Watching videos, attending webinars, and doing online courses is all great, but if you don't start moving, you won't get anywhere. You have to be careful that learning doesn't turn into procrastination. It's great to want to continue to learn, but if you are only acquiring knowledge and not actually implementing what you learn, you are not going to change anything.

You need to learn the rule of the game: Don't wait until you are ready to start, because the truth is that you will never be ready. Life is full of stages, and there is always something you are not ready for. So start now, and make the one move. One move is all it takes. When you move, life shifts.

Be ready. Fire. Aim! It's that simple. Planning too much might actually ignite fear and keep you stuck. Always align yourself, remember your goals before taking action, and avoid making decisions from a place of lack.

It's important to relax and do less too. You are always so busy "doing" that often you miss the signs showing that you are going in the wrong direction. Sometimes you need to slow down and let your soul catch up.

Before you make your move, ask yourself, "Am I feeling the feeling that supports what I am about to do?" Doing this will save you time and headaches. If things are not happening the way you want them to, you can be sure that nothing you do will change that. You will need to stop whatever it is you are trying to do, until the way you are feeling about it changes.

When I see my clients struggling with taking aligned action, and I can feel they are getting frustrated, I tell them to go do something else. I always suggest having multiple things that you can work on simultaneously. That way, if you feel you are starting to switch modes, you can drop it right there, go work on something else, and come back to it when your mind has released those emotions that were making you feel stuck. It always works!

If you are getting frustrated because you are not getting something right, stop doing it but come back to it at a later time. Any fear-based action is not aligned action; there also shouldn't be any rush. Let your heart lead you, not your mind. When the action is leading you to what is for you, your body will feel relaxed but energized, and in flow.

When you start to match what you desire with your feelings, and take actions to match that, you create new habits. If your desires and goals seem too big or too far, you can start with small goals that will lead you there. The important thing is to keep moving.

If you already had the life you want, what would you be doing right now? What habits would you have? Using them expands your power, so start doing those. Start creating habits in your life as if you were already that person.

Begin with 10 minutes a day. Be the person you have always wanted to be. If you are too shy, start talking to strangers when you go out. If the problem is guilt, do something to feel approved. If the problem is that you think the world doesn't notice you, do something aligned with your purpose, and you will be seen and heard. Now is the time to not only create a new habit but to become her, the real you.

The Power of Intention

Say yes to your reality. When you set intentions, you give your subconscious directions. Everything that has happened started with a decision or a choice you made.

You have created your current reality. It all started with a thought, feeling, image, or an intention you once had.
Decide on one thing that you really really want. Without an intent, you will have a hard time creating your ideal life. You need to know what you want, and commit yourself to the things that will get you closer to achieving it.

Your intentions have to be believable for you. I always tell my coaching clients to start with things they believe they can do but that are not too easy to achieve. It should be somewhere in the middle. Make it attainable and adjustable.

I love using "I decree and declare" statements; it carries a very strong power behind it, like a commitment that cannot be broken. If you use words like "want" and "need," you are saying that you don't have it, and speaking from a place of lack will bring you more lack.

After you set your intentions for the day, you let them be. Release complete control. If you keep thinking about it, your mind may start to doubt. It could lead to overthinking about it and, instead, you will be sending out signals that you don't trust the Universe. You don't have to think about how you are going to achieve them.

Intention is like a seed that is creating your future. You don't plant a seed and doubt if it will grow, do you? You also don't plant an apple seed and expect a pear tree to grow. You just know and trust that you will get what you are planting. Your job is to see it, feel it, and believe it. Life will handle the rest.

Always speak your intentions in the present tense, just like your incantations. And obviously, you want to say it in a positive, loving tone. Feeling the reality of your intentions, as if it already happened, helps you identify opportunities and things you would have not noticed otherwise.

Remember how powerful your words are, and avoid using words like "try," "will stop," "will not," etc. You want to focus on what you will do, have, and be. So instead of saying, "I will try to not eat processed food," you could say something like, "I intend that my body be healthy and full of energy. I choose to eat what nurtures my body."

If you are still having doubts, play the worst-case scenario game again, until you release resistance. Would you be okay if it didn't happen? Let go by accepting the opposite or worst-case scenario. Most likely, the worst-case scenario is very similar to your situation right now.

Stay loyal to it! There is no need to create a plan B. If you are creating a plan B in case your plan doesn't work, you are emitting a lack of trust. Feel it, see it, and trust that it is done.

You can practice setting intentions to get used to how it works. Start by telling yourself what you are about to do before you do it. Train your mind. Your intentions should feel the same way as when you walk from a room in your home to another. You don't question if you are going to do it; you just do it.

Add more power to it by seeing in your mind how your day is going to unfold, by looking at it from different angles and through other people's eyes.

Right before you go to sleep is a powerful time to create. Think about tomorrow and how you want your day to be. Imagine the perfect day and waking up happy and full of energy, and you will.

Can You See It?

Imagination is the world of grown-up kids living in the land of make believe. It's being able to see and accept the link between the visible and the invisible. Practice using it. One of your highest gifts is the ability to imagine something that is not in your physical reality yet. Decide what it is that you want; then go about creating it.

Think of an image. Make it come to life. Where is it? Who is there? What do you smell? Is it cold?

Think childhood. Recall events, people, and food.

What does your dream home look like? Cut out or print pictures similar to your vision. Visualize a party. Walk around the home; what do you see? Go do some work in the garden. Do things around the home. Invite guests. What are they saying to you? How many bedrooms does your home have? Can you see the sunrise? Is there a lake? How many cars can you fit in the driveway? Is it in the city? Who lives there? What type of furniture do you have? What is that scent you smell every time you walk into your home? What are you having for dinner tonight? Who is cooking? Is there anything you want to change? Maybe you need a new couch. Where are you putting it?

Did you feel that? I love using my imagination and playing make believe. I can recall so many times when I visualized things down to the smallest details and actually got them, especially in regard to homes, like the noise my backdoor made and how I wanted to live by the water, and how a real estate agent friend happened to take me to see a home that I originally said was too far, but when I went to see it, I fell in love with it.

It matched my visualization to a t. It had such a strong personality and a beautiful backyard. One of my best friends even had his wedding there. It was beautiful. Not only did it come with a Jacuzzi, but it was also minutes walking distance from the lake. It wasn't planned at all, nor was it the location I originally wanted. It was actually totally in the opposite direction of where I had in mind. The Universe delivered, and not just that time; the same thing happened with my next 2 homes.

When visualizing your house, walk in it, open the windows, and put groceries away. Every time I did visualization when looking for a house, I realized afterwards how much the things I imagined matched my reality.

On my last move, I remember imagining a house with more room for my boys. I remember seeing my kitchen with a fridge big enough to fit food for 3 teenagers and my fiancé. It's funny but I couldn't fit my groceries in a regular-size fridge. It wasn't a big deal; I just had to buy groceries more often. I didn't even think much of it. When I went to an open house at my current home, I couldn't stop laughing when I saw the double door fridge. It is literally the size of two fridges combined.

Similar to the previous home, I wanted to either live by the lake or have a hot tub, so I pictured asking the boys why the floors in the kitchen were wet. The last home we had, came with a beautiful oasis backyard, with an inground pool and a waterfall.

Will the Real You Please Stand Up

Walk into your closet, and see yourself deciding which outfit you are going to wear for your party tonight. Have fun with it.

Can you, for a moment, imagine that you have a million dollars? If you can't imagine it, it will be difficult to have it. Do it, even if it is just for fun. How would you spend that money? Would you go on vacation? Whom would you take? Would you invest it in a new business you have been wanting to start? How about donations? Whom would you help?

Close your eyes and imagine the best version of yourself possible. That's who you really are. THE REAL YOU! Get rid of any part of you that doesn't believe it.

Visualize it in the way that a mom watches her child grow, with "heart eyes." Rehearsing it in your mind allows you to connect to a part of your mind that you don't normally have access to. Your subconscious is more powerful when you think in pictures than when using words.

It's extremely powerful if you use all your 5 senses, and if the images are felt. When you can see it and feel yourself having it, it's a hint that you are capable of having it.
In case you have already started saying to yourself that you are not creative and can't visualize, I am going to stop you right there. Everyone can!

Imagine a pink elephant in the room. What do you see? Exactly!

Thinking the thought and picturing in your mind is visualization.

Travel: Imagine exotic places; see yourself booking your flight. Is there a beach? Who is with you? Have you been there before? Don't forget to take lots of selfies! Are you staying in a hotel, or did you book an Airbnb?

Try to not leave anything out. Visualize all areas in your life. All areas need to be working together. One impacts the other. Each area is a part of you. All of them together become who you are, and oh boy! I can't wait to see the day you meet the real you.

As you start practicing visualization, you will notice that your ideas and your thoughts will start to change, and you will notice your reality adjusting to it. Imagine the world you want to create, and go about creating it. And that's how you vibrate at the same frequency as what you want. At that point, you become unstoppable.

One of my clients was having difficulties with her teenage son. I suggested that she use visualization and imagine her reality with her son, manifesting his potential and becoming all that he could be, and loving him and accepting him the way he was.

A few weeks later, I received a call from her to tell me that things had started to change quickly, and that their relationship had started to get better. She said that visualization had helped her release control and let things flow.

If there is an area that you are not satisfied with, forget about it now. Start to tell a new story, and believe in it. If you keep looking at the things you dislike, you will find more things to dislike. Focus on the things you like!

> *"The only thing keeping you from what you want*
> *is what you tell yourself."*
> **– Tony Robbins**

The Stories You Tell Yourself

You have to start by taking responsibility for your life, and stop blaming others for everything that happens in your life. Regain control by stopping the victim game. Stop whining and complaining about the current situation; claim the opposite.

Start by realizing how you talk to yourself and about yourself.

Reduce your reaction to the situations you experience. I will give you an example. Let say you just woke up and went to the kitchen to make yourself a yummy cup of coffee. When you went to reach for the sugar in your cabinet, you hit your head on the corner of the cabinet door. It hurt! What did you do? Did you grab your cell and start calling all your friends to tell them what happened? Did you talk about how life was unfair and it shouldn't have happened to you?

Now let's imagine a different scenario. This time, you were not alone. You went to the grocery store and, as you were walking down the toilet paper aisle, a 5-year-old came running and stepped on your toes. What did you do? Did you grab your phone again and write a huge post about it on social media, for everyone to see and understand what you were going through?

I bet you didn't make a big deal about either scenario. You just went on and kept living your life as if they didn't even happen.

Did you go around speaking about the cabinet all day? I am sure you didn't. So why would you act that way when you experience other things in life? They don't define you—they are all just experiences—but the way you react to them does. Your reaction to the experiences impacts your life.

If you want to change your reality, you need to start taking responsibility for everything in your life. If it's there, it's because you put it there. The only way to choose a new reality is to first accept your current one.

The truth is, it is what it is. By accepting it, you lower the importance.

Stop making excuses for not doing the things you want to be doing. The most common excuse I hear from my clients is a lack of time. Waiting until you have time will never create time. It's just a lie you tell yourself. We all get the same amount of time in the day; it's what you choose to do with it that counts. Start scheduling time to do the things that are important to you, and use the time you have left to do the other things.

Negative and unwanted things will keep showing up until you stop saying that you don't want them. Stop talking about them. Rewrite your story.

Dr. Wayne Dyer told a story once about his friend writing the story of her life in 5 chapters. I thought it was so powerful, and I always share it with my clients.

A Life in 5 Chapters by Portia Nelson

Chapter 1
I walk down the street.
There is a deep hole in the sidewalk.
I fall in.
I am lost... I am helpless.
It isn't my fault.
It takes forever to find a way out.

Chapter 2
I walk down the same street.
There is a deep hole in the sidewalk.
I pretend I don't see it.

I fall in again.
I can't believe I am in the same place.
But it isn't my fault.
It still takes me a long time to get out.

Chapter 3
I walk down the same street.
There is a deep hole in the sidewalk.
I see it is there.
I still fall in. It's a habit.
My eyes are open.
I know where I am.
It is my fault. I get out immediately.

Chapter 4
I walk down the same street.
There is a deep hole in the sidewalk.
I walk around it.

Chapter 5
I walk down another street.

Someone with a victim mentality is always living in reaction mode and blaming others for everything. Whatever you give too much attention to gets stronger. Fighting against it has the same power as fighting for it. Don't let things take you off balance.

Fear, guilt, and an inferiority complex are other emotions to which if you keep paying attention, will keep you on the path with more traps and holes.

What can you do to stop telling those stories that keep you stuck?

See and accept that there is a giant hole in the ground.
Know that you can go around it.

Just because it's there, it doesn't have to affect you at all.
Relax; accept its existence.
And keep moving. Take a different road.

If you think it's having effects on you, see yourself as a third person in the story, and observe the situation from a different angle. You will notice that by removing emotions, and keeping yourself unattached to situations, it will allow you to see different paths. Reduce reactions and release emotions, and the path will get clear.

Mission Statement

Now that you know your goals, desires, and purpose, let's create your mission statement. Ask yourself what you think your mission is.

Your mission statement defines who you are. It identifies your purpose in life, and it explains what you intend to do or offer to make it happen, and why it is important to you. It is your reason for being, and the key to finding your path in life.

I suggest you keep it short and simple—one to two sentences long.
I think everyone should create a mission statement, regardless if they are a stay-at- home mom, an entrepreneur, a coach, or a student. It helps you to stay focused on what you want, and to make decisions by checking if what you are about to do matches your goals.

You can't get this wrong. It's basically a way to put your purpose or calling into words. Once you have created your statement, start using it. Place a copy of it everywhere. It's a great tool to always remind you of who you are, what you are here to do, and why.

It's also a fantastic way to inform others of what your intentions are. I find that others will offer to help you accomplish it, or they will move out of your way.

Will the Real You Please Stand Up

Let's look at some examples of mission statements from people that have become successful and achieved their goals.

> "My mission in life is not merely to survive, but to thrive; and to do so with some passion, some compassion, some humor, and some style."
> – Maya Angelou

> "To be a teacher, and to be known for inspiring my students to be more than they thought they could be."
> – Oprah Winfrey

> "To have fun in my journey through life and learn from my mistakes."
> – Richard Branson

How about you? What do you want to be remembered for?

What legacy do you want to leave behind?
Where do you see yourself in 5, 10, 20 years?

How are you going to make an impact?

Your mission doesn't have to be a world-changing kind of mission; nothing is ever too little.

I will share with you my mission statement.

> "To lead the way by going first, and impact lives by sharing my experiences and my words. What I want for myself, I want for everyone else. I am committed to expressing the real me so that others can also see all the possibilities in themselves."
> – Bee Soars

Chapter 4

#CATCHUPTOHER

"Your vision will become clear only when you can look into your own heart. Who looks outside, dreams; who looks inside, awakes."
– Carl Jung

www.willtherealyou.com

Pixie, the Adorable Active Little One

It's time to call your mini-you to come out and play! I remember reading somewhere that 6 out of 10 kids didn't receive the love they needed as a child, and they were raised by loving parents.

Let's repair your relationship with your inner child and heal those wounds. They could've been caused by something that was only serious and hurtful because they were lived and experienced through your childlike mind, or by physical or psychological abuse, or maybe a broken family.

Your mini-you seeks protection, and is vulnerable and afraid. She wants to be loved and wants to belong.

You need to make her feel that she can trust you, and that you will always protect her so that she can start to heal herself. Self-love starts here by loving her. All she wants is to be loved and respected. Maybe you had a healthy, happy childhood, but a friend moved away and you felt heartbroken and abandoned. Maybe you were bullied at school; kids can be so mean.

Whatever the case was, you most likely have some wounds from childhood, and if you don't heal them now, you will keep getting triggered when life brings you experiences with similar emotions waiting to be released. Regardless of the intensity of the new experiences, the same pain you experienced as a child will be felt again.

Will the Real You Please Stand Up

With my clients, I always start the inner child work by asking them to draw their mini-selves with their non-dominant hand, and truly experience the emotion of a child while drawing. The best way to do this is to use lots of colors and add emotions. Is she happy or sad? Where is she? Is she holding a toy? What is she doing? Is she at home or at the park?

Next, I tell them to have a conversation with her. Ask her questions. Some of my clients prefer to do this in meditation. But you can also write her a letter or have a conversation; again, using your non-dominant hand to let her respond.

Listening and understanding your inner child is very important for you to grow. Let her know that she is loved and that you will always protect her. Find out how she is feeling and what makes her happy. What does she need? Try to remember what you liked to do when you were little.

These exercises will help heal childhood wounds that could have been incorrectly created through your childlike perspective of the world.

This can be lots of fun! Some of my clients have incorporated this into their lives, and whenever they feel any negative emotions, they go back to their inner child and have a talk with her.

Think of all the things you used to do as a child, and do them. I am sure she would love that. There are so many things you can do. You can play, draw, or dance. Go see nature. Take a walk on the beach. Sing. It will make her happy and will help you stay young, love yourself, and connect with your real self. Be a childlike spirit with adult power.

If it helps, look at photos of yourself as a child. Nurture her. Let her know that you love her, and that you are sorry for anything that might have made her sad. Ask her to forgive you, and thank her. Let her know that you are there for her and that she is safe.

This exercise will help you connect with the part of your mind that is childlike, curious, and innocent.

Practice self-care as if you were your own parent. Start by setting some boundaries. Go to bed early. Take a bath and listen to relaxing music. Use some essential oils and get a massage. Cook a yummy, healthy meal. How about giving yourself a treat?

What is the one thing you most want to say to your inner child today?

Rebella, the Beautiful Rebellious Girl

A few years have passed. Hurray!!! You are finally a teenager. With that, you also got doubts, new emotions, heartbreaks, a million questions, and the desire to fit in somewhere, along with others wanting you to feel less pretty, less smart, and less talented.

Think back to when you were her. Connect with her. She still lives within you. How does she feel?

Let her tell you all her beliefs and worries. Remembering your teen years will give you access to a part of your life you may have forgotten.

Help her make peace with the choices she made. Help her find all her beliefs, especially the most false ones, and guide her to recreate them by replacing them with more encouraging ones.

It's in the teen years—through our experiences, mistakes, breakups, and failure—that we create most of the false beliefs we carry with us.

These beliefs limit us from achieving our dreams and desires. It keeps us in our comfort zone, avoiding pain, failures, and disappointments. Most of these beliefs are not real and need to be replaced with empowering ones.

Think back to when you were a teen. Write everything down in your journal. Imagine you are going for a walk with your teen self. Talk to her. Ask her questions. Wait for the answers.

What is important to you? What is not?

Is there anything wrong?

How does it make you feel?

What can I do to make sure it doesn't happen again?

I put together a list with the most common things my clients have given, as examples, to help you create your own list. If you can relate, write them down and try to come up with different meanings for each of them.

Words describing negative attitudes can creep into your mind and, when they do, it's hard to get them out. Flipping the phrases to include a solution will make you shift how you felt when you first heard the statements.

I don't like your hair.
New meaning: I love your confidence.

You are so childish and immature.
New meaning: You always know how to have fun.

Speak up; I can't hear you.
New meaning: I really want to know how you feel about it.

- Be quiet; you are too loud.
- You are too much.
- Those are nonsense feelings.
- Stupid.
- You are so ungrateful.
- You are not going out dressed like that.
- Who do you think you are?
- You don't know anything.
- You look like a bum dressed like that.
- I don't like your attitude.
- You don't have a reason to be crying.
- That's a dumb choice.
- It's one problem after another with you.
- You are so lazy.
- If you don't like the rules, you can leave.
- You are so selfish.

Let her know that you are there for her. Find out her worries and dreams. Love her for who she is. She is just trying to be accepted and is caught in between identities. Let her know that everything will be okay.

Enchantress, the Charming Romantic Healer

There is more to the truth than just the facts, and the Enchantress knows. She is all about the Divine feminine energy.

She is that charming, magical, mystical, and confident woman. She is a fascinating woman with all the answers.

She is a student of life, and her words are her power. She manipulates magical energy using her words.

She invites you to go deep and reinvent yourself, over and over as you wish.

She guides you to face your limiting beliefs and fears, and to not be afraid as she is always with you.

She takes you to meet who you truly are. There is never any logic in what she tells you, but you can feel the truth down to your bones.

She shows you how to release pain, guilt, and suffering. She will lead you and show you how to develop your unique powers.

She is not timid; she is charming.

She is discreet but powerful.

Need guidance? Talk to her.

Want to know your next move? Ask her.

Want to develop your powers? Embody her.

Grab your journal. Request and intend to receive the answers for your questions. Write them all down. Use your right hand for the questions, and your left hand for the answers. By using both hands, it will trigger the intuitive side of your brain—the feminine side, which is creative, delicate, intuitive, and receptive—the part of you that just knows without an explanation. Its roots reach deep into the heart.

Let the answers come. Don't worry about spelling, punctuation, or grammar—just write.

Journaling

"What is written with a pen cannot be cut down with an axe."
– Russian proverb

Your soul and body come together and become a unit when you not only think about something but also declare it in writing.

I used to struggle to keep a diary. I couldn't remember to do it. Some days I had so much to say, while other days, nothing... I actually completed my first diary when I started writing this book. I was so proud, and now I can't go a day without it.

Have you ever tried to explain a thought you had but couldn't express it in words?

There are so many benefits to writing a journal, and that's one of them—the more you write, the more clarity you receive. Your mind gets clear, and you find answers. It's a wonderful way to vent without worrying about what others are going to say.

It makes you feel listened to.

So start writing; let the words flow. Get to know yourself better—just write.

Free writing is what some call channeling, and others call it downloads.

Here are some journaling prompts to get you started.

- Whom can I help today?
- How can I solve an issue today?
- What should I do next to grow my business?
- What is the one move I can make right now that will get me closer to my goals?
- What is my subconscious trying to tell me?
- How can I be better today than I was yesterday?
- What is the path of least resistance?
- What can I celebrate today?
- What is keeping me from my outcomes?
- Is what I am about to do helping me with my goals?
- What limiting beliefs am I responding to?
- Is what I am worried about now, important in the future?
- Is worrying about the current situation going to change anything?
- Are the thoughts I am thinking about, what I want to create in my life?
- What memory was triggered just now?

I have always been the kind of person that likes to write things down, and I don't mean by typing it on my laptop or cell—I mean actually using a pen and a paper. There is something truly magical about it. What if I said that you can create the life you want by simply writing it down?

Chapter 5

Ditch the Crabs

*"If you are brave enough to say goodbye,
life will reward you with a new hello."*
– Paulo Coelho

Words You Speak

The ability to use words is the most powerful tool we have as humans. It's really like magic—well, they are magic. You can use them to heal or to destroy. Whatever I say to you will make you feel and think. Anything you say will impact your reality.

There is a big difference between being nice and being kind. You should always be kind. Learning to communicate with others and yourself is one of the most powerful things you can do.

Being nice is when you are polite and treat people with respect. *Kind* is different; when you are kind, it shows you care. It's easy to be nice. To be kind, you need to see yourself in others, in order to understand them and connect.

I have always made a big deal about the words used inside my home. My kids are well aware of how words work. I not only tell them about the power of words, but I show them too.

When they were little, I remember hearing someone on TV say that there are 9 minutes that are very important in a child's day: the first 3 minutes when they wake up, 3 minutes after school, and the 3 minutes before they go to sleep.

To this day, I make sure the words they hear from me at those times are words that will make them feel loved and special. Even when we do get into disagreements, I laugh and say at the end, "I am still a bit upset, but I always love you," and the best part is that they always say it back, even if in a text message.

It doesn't matter whom you are talking to—whether it's your teen or a stranger on the street. Treat everyone as an old friend. People like who likes them. If you want them to respect you, don't wait for it. Treat them the way you want to be treated. If they are family, it's an even bigger reason to do so—make them feel that in your eyes, they are important.

For better or for worse, your life is always responding to the words you say. It's extremely important to clean up your vocabulary. If you use words in a negative way, it hurts you and others. Stop complaining and gossiping. Words are like codes you are activating. Your reality is always a mix of your words and beliefs.

You are human, and you will most definitely say things that you don't mean when life ignites your emotions. Bringing awareness to the moment will help you. Let your emotions flow. Feel the feeling, but make sure you take time before you do or say anything to act on those emotions.

Start being aware of the story you tell yourself. Can you tell your story without negative words? From now on, see if you can tell your stories and leave out words of pain and wounds.

Pay attention to how you talk to others. Do you empower them with the words you speak, or not? I notice that a lot of people struggle to use words to empower others. This is not their fault. They simply were not taught this.

Children learn an average of 6000 words a year. Knowing this, I have always made sure that my boys knew how to always choose the words that made them feel good to say, and which would do the same for the people hearing them, especially if they were using words to describe others.

Listen to the words spoken in your home. How do they make you feel? If they are not words that make you feel good, shift them to better feeling ones. Home energy is so important; it is where you spend most of your time. I have always been very clear on protecting the energy in my home, especially with the choices of words we use.

When you use the word "need," for example, it's coming from *not having*, from experiencing a lack of something. Instead of "need," saying "want" would be better, because that comes from desiring it.

If you speak and think that something will be a struggle, it will be. Instead, say that it will all work out, and it will. Trust it! Eliminate words like "trying." All trying does is to invite difficulties to come your way. Trying means that you are not going to succeed; you will just try. Why even bother to do something if you are not going to give your all? If you are going to do something, just say that you are doing it. That is it!

- Everything you say yes to, you give power.
- Everything you say no to, you also give power.

If you choose to keep talking about how life is hard and difficult, you will keep finding and attracting people with the same vibe to talk about these things. How does that make you feel when you complain and keep telling others the stories of everything that went wrong in your life?

You need to realize that everything and everyone that shows up in your life are a match to your vibration, being the words you are speaking or emotions you are transmitting. You attract friends and relationships that are experiencing things at the same frequency.

When two people are no longer a match, they usually go their separate ways. It doesn't mean you should go around feeling you are better than others because you know something they don't know. Everyone is moving at their own speed, and feeling that you are better than others will lower your vibration. Mind your business. What others do or say is not your business. Your business is to focus on your life, and be impeccable with your words.

The Lies You Tell Yourself

There is a chance that you have actually tried to change your life and go after your goals, and have failed. Maybe you have even given up because you think you have tried everything. If you can relate to this, I am sorry to tell you but you might have a case of limiting beliefs. This is a serious problem. Think of it as a virus that has taken control of your mind, and it affects how you think, behave, and act. It can also impact how you connect and relate to others. Even worse, they can make your mind foggy and unclear, making you confuse these beliefs with the truth.

A belief is what you tell yourself to be true. They can be positive and help you grow, or be negative and keep you stuck. Most people mistake these limiting beliefs for the truth. Most of these limitations were imposed on you by society, family, and friends. They are fake beliefs and are not based on actual facts.

All your worries, ideas about life, limitations, and fears were created from the perception your child mind had, when you had an untouched program and you were your original self—before you began adjusting to those around you.

Throughout life, we hear and see situations that without even noticing, they end up being impregnated in our minds, and we take them as absolute truths.

Digital marketing experts estimate that in North America, the average person is exposed to around 4000 to 10000 ads per day, and without even knowing it, those images are being imprinted in your subconscious, and you end up thinking those images belong to you.

A big example of this was people believing they had to hoard and stack things because there wasn't going to be enough during the Covid19 lockdown.

You end up living someone else's thoughts. No wonder, even when you achieve your goals, you are not happy.

Limiting beliefs can also come as masks we wear in order to get approved. To grow, you need to understand that's not you. Everyone in your life leaves a fingerprint on your unconscious mind.

What is a belief? A belief is just a statement you believe to be true. It doesn't mean it is. You can't see it. It doesn't have any shape or color. Beliefs are created in two ways: by your experiences or by accepting what others tell you to be the truth. Most of them are formed when you are small and have a childlike mind.

When kids are criticized, they grow up to think that they are not enough. When kids receive no affection, they grow up to think that they are not worth loving. When kids receive no attention, they grow up to think that they are not important. These beliefs become the lies you tell yourself.

It does not mean that they come from bad parenting; it's just the way you interpreted something that you experienced in your life, and without awareness, those became your core beliefs, and you live life by them.

If you are a mom, I recommend that every time you have an interaction with your child, you should stop to think how she felt when she walked away from you. Do you want her to believe that what just happened is how life is supposed to be? A belief you want her to create? If not, this is your chance to fix it. Allow your children to see that you are human too, and that you are learning with them.

What can you do since you are not a child anymore and all your beliefs have been fully created? Don't worry; all is not lost. First, you need to know what your core beliefs are.

The quickest way to find out if you have "LBS" (limiting beliefs)—and most of us do—is to notice themes in your thinking. It could be an area in your life that doesn't seem to be working, and you don't do anything about it because you don't believe it can be improved. Your inner world needs to change before your outer world does.

You can imagine everything you want, but if you don't believe you can and will have it all, or that you are not capable or deserving of it, you are going to keep not having it. A negative way of thinking cannot create a positive future.

The good news is that you don't have to feel disappointed and lose hope. Once you acknowledge these lies you keep telling yourself, you bring them from your subconscious to your conscious, making it easy to get rid of them and reprogram your mind with what you want instead.

How do you do it???

Simple. You turn the switch on and flip them. You change the script that has been written for you.

We usually have these beliefs on autopilot, and you have to understand that everything around you was created from beliefs you have. It's all a perception. You start by choosing new filters to see reality, if you want to change it.

Life is always bringing you situations that match how you view the world. If you believe that life is hard, life will be hard. These beliefs influence how you feel, which influences your behaviors, which gives you results.

You are going to have to let go of a lot of things to unlock that next level in your life. Just like an onion, you will need to peel it back to find lies and images. Go through all layers. Areas of money and love are usually where you will find the strongest beliefs.

Here is a list to help you identify the most common ones.

- I am not good enough.
- I am too old to start over.
- I don't have the body to wear the clothes I want.
- I don't have time.
- I won't find love as a single mom.
- This is how I am; I can't change.
- I can't do it; I don't know how.
- I can't afford this.
- I will never achieve my goals.
- I am not smart enough.
- You have to work hard for your money.
- I don't deserve to be happy.
- It's not possible to make money doing what you love.
- I will never find love.
- It's too late for me.
- I can't get a better job because I don't have a degree.
- No one ever chooses me.
- I am too shy.
- If I am too friendly, others will think I am flirting.
- You have to work hard if you want to be rich.
- People wouldn't want to learn from me.
- I have an accent.
- English is not my first language; they won't understand me.

- I am new; no one is going to want to pay me for my services.

Start questioning everything. Bring awareness to all areas of your life. Argue with your mind. What is blocking you from seeing things for what they truly are? Observe things instead of reacting to them. Choose a new belief.

What do you believe to be true about yourself? Money? Relationships? Body? What limiting beliefs are you responding to?

How can you flip them? If you think you are too old to get fit, start telling yourself that it's not too late to start, and commit yourself to go for a 15-minute walk every day until you create a new habit.

In my coaching programs, we go deep into this. It's the hardest work, and it's never done. It's an ongoing process. These beliefs are unknown until you become aware of them, but once you acknowledge their existence, it becomes easier to flip them when you get triggered by one.

These toxic beliefs can impact your entire existence and block you where there should be unlimited potential. You need to get rid of them. They have no power than the power you give them. How much do you believe them? It's time to develop a new reality, with belief in the potential that lies within you.

Make your new beliefs real; say them out loud, and support them with action. If you believe that you are intelligent and smart, act accordingly.

Fears are Prayers for What You Don't Want

If you study people that are successful, you will find out they achieved success because they were not afraid of expressing themselves as themselves.

They didn't let the idea of what people could think of them stop them. Were they afraid? Of course they were; they are human. But that's the secret about fears. Instead of running away and avoiding things that scare you, you chase it as if it's actually what you desire.

You don't go in the opposite direction of fear; you go after it, look at it, and face it. When you face it, magic happens, and all the things you were scared of disappear; opportunities show up to help you become your true self. This is how your identity starts to shift.

Life places the best things in life on the other side of fear.

Fear is an internal alarm made to protect us; however, fear lies. Your mind wants to protect you and keep you safe, and it's always looking for ways you could get hurt. It simply wants to make sure your basic needs are met, like shelter and food, and that you are not going to be jumped on by a bear, or clawed to death by a giant tiger. Ninety percent of your fears will most likely never manifest.

For thousands of years, the brain did its best to protect us and to make us afraid of things that could logically kill us. When we lived in caves, these fears kept us safe.

Nobody is trying to kill you now, and we live in a pretty safe place (mostly). However, our brains still operate in the same way.

What I get asked a lot is how to know the difference between your inner guidance and other voices—whether the voice is coming from your internal GPS or from the limiting beliefs imposed on you by family, friends, and society.

Your inner guidance comes from a place that wants you to experience growth and love. It's that first voice you hear before your mind comes in and starts labeling things and using logic. It's sweet and all about love. It gives you one answer—no need for an explanation.

Your mind and limiting beliefs sound different, and they will make you think and believe that you can't do things and that you shouldn't try.

The only fear that is valid is when you are in physical danger. Most of your fears, worries, self-doubts, and limiting beliefs were created from the perception of your mind as a child, and most likely not with the right perception.

- Your heart always knows.
- Your mind thinks it knows.
- But it's your heart that guides you the right way.

What do you think your limitations are?

Are they preventing you from doing something different?

Take a minute and think about what you have always wanted to do. Are you doing it right now?

What are you afraid of?

What is holding you back?

You spend so much time worrying, and most of the time those things you worry about never even cross your reality. It's good to know that your worries most likely will never become a reality; however, you still waste your energy worrying and overthinking about these imaginary things.

A quick way to reduce your anxiety when dealing with fear is to take a few minutes and play the "then what" game by trying to think of the worst thing that could actually happen. Don't do it for too long; 5 minutes or so is enough. You don't want to put any type of energy into it. If this thing that is causing you to stress were to happen, what would your life be like? Would it change much from what it is now?

Once you know what the worst thing is that could actually happen, and most of the time doesn't even happen, you calm down. If you know what the worst-case scenario is, and what it will make you feel like, you can stop acting as if this thing is happening now. It's not actually happening, so why act as if it is?

Most of the time, the worst-case scenario is actually your current life. I started using this technique with my boys when they were little. Not only did we have fun playing it, but it also helped them to get over their fears. Now I do it with my private clients, and I have watched them transform.

Start by asking yourself:

- What are you afraid of?
- Is your worst-case scenario really likely to happen?
- If it actually happened, then what?
- Then what?
- Then what?

There is no "then what"; there is only "now," and if there is no giant tiger waiting for you outside, there is really nothing stopping you—nada.

Get Comfortable Feeling Uncomfortable

It's when you get that feeling and the desire to change, and you decide that you no longer want to stay in your comfort zone, that you are ready to transform.

Give yourself a little push to leave fear behind, and imagine how your life will change if you live the life you want. Think about all the things you will get out of it if you do this, and all the things you will lose if you don't. Most people get stuck on the fears of losing what they have, and that gets in their way.

Most of the transformations happen when people hit rock bottom or have a tragedy happen in their lives. At that point, you have nothing to lose and everything to gain. You don't have to wait for something bad to happen to transform your life; you can start now.

All it takes is a decision, one move. Everything you have in your life was already created by you. Your current life is a result of the choices and decisions you made in your past. If you did it once, you can do it again. We already know you can create the things you now have.

It's time to create new things, a new life, a new you. To create new things, you have to do new things; otherwise, you will keep creating the same experiences. How can you do that? Do the unexpected.

Do something that is very awkward until it feels normal. Explore new things; get rid of the old. What does your new version of yourself do? Do that!

Throw yourself in the river at 4 a.m. if you have to. I did. I was stubbornly holding onto what was familiar to me, and it was only when I started moving, making new choices, that my life started to change.

You will never experience any growth and change if you keep doing the same things over and over. You have to move. One move; that's all it takes to get the flow going.

When you start to walk out of your comfort zone, people will question you. Some might even try to stop you, because they don't understand and just want to keep you safe. Most likely, when you start to leave your comfort zone, you will start to have some doubt.

Ignore your fears and do it anyway. Ignore your self-limitations, your doubts, and even the people. You will realize that you had the master key to your life this entire time. None of that will happen if you don't start to move now. Don't sit around on the couch doing nothing. Get up! You need to start taking aligned action—massive action.

The world is waiting for you. When you make the decision to do something different, you are not only changing your world but the world of everyone else around you. Think about your why; the reason you want to change your life. Your why will give you the strength to do it. If your why is not bigger than your fears, you don't have the right reasons.

Clean up Your Clutter

You want new things to come to your life, but you have no room for them. There is no better way to shift your energy and raise your frequency than decluttering your life.

Before you can call abundance into your life, you need to make room for it so that you are ready to receive it. Start physically preparing for them to arrive. If you know and trust that they are coming, the best way to be ready is to make room for them.

Will the Real You Please Stand Up

Look around your inner and outer space. Decide what is working for you and what is not.

Walk around your home and remove everything that feels like it doesn't belong or match the vibe of the person you choose to become. Get rid of it!

If you are like most people, you have tons of things that you got decades ago when you were a different person, and most likely not a reflection of the person you are today. Get rid of them, and release that old energy!

Only buy things that match the next version of yourself.

Go through your closet and start donating the clothes you have been saving for a special occasion, but the right occasion never seems to come. I bet you have a few outfits you are saving that if you try them on, they are either too big or too small. If you haven't used it in 3 months, or if it's something that carries emotional baggage, get rid of it. The best and only rule to follow is the "wear it or eliminate it" rule.

How about the perfume or lotion you are saving for when you go out, which has been sitting in your drawer? Yeah, the one that most likely has lost the original scent and now smells old and stale, or like a fake version that they sell at a dollar store. Believe it or not, I had a perfume that was 20 years old; a high school boyfriend had given it to me on Valentine's Day.

Why aren't you using it? Are you not worth it? Are you scared that you will never find another to replace it? That comes from a lack mentality. Does it do you any good to save it and take up space? You are saving it, but you are also not using it, so why even have it?

This needs to stop, and please do it now. When you do this, you are blocking yourself from receiving more. You are acting from a place of lack, and that will keep you in the same spot.

There is a higher frequency when your home feels organized and cleaned. Keep only things that work. I love that feeling. I am one of those people that when the cleaner comes to clean my house, I have already cleaned and organized everything. When I organize my home, I organize my mind.

The same goes for relationships. Are you looking for a relationship and haven't found anyone that would be the ideal match to the image you have? Let's say you found the one. Would he/she be moving in? Would you even have space in your closet?

How about your wallet? When was the last time you cleaned it? Is it full of receipts and expired gift cards? Is there even room for money?

Energy Vampires

When I talk about decluttering your life, I am talking about all areas, including the people you have around. Until you are at a point in your life where other people's negativity doesn't affect you, you need to stay away from them.

It's better to spend time alone than to be with those that have a victim mentality or those that hold you back. But it's also important to remember that if that's the type of people that you are attracting, the problem is not them but you.

If these are the type of people that are showing up in your life, it's because you are offering the same vibration; after all, like attracts like. So, most likely, you are being negative or playing the victim card without even noticing it. Being yourself filters those that don't belong in your life, and shows you the ones that do.

It's okay if you don't have a lot of friends; if anything, that will actually make it easier. Instead of walking away from people that don't bring positive things into your life, you can just go out there and make new ones.

You want to be around people that uplift you and believe in you. You don't necessarily need to know them personally. They could even be friends you have online. I have actually met some awesome people that have turned into amazing friends, through social media.

Take an audit of your close relationships. How do you feel when you are around them? Do they make you laugh? Do they make you comfortable being yourself? You want to be around people that are living the life you want. We become the people we hang out with. Surround yourself with people that will help you grow.

Have the kind of friends you would want your kids to have. Would your friends be the type of friends you would want for your kids?

Creating a Personal Inventory

Creating a personal inventory is very helpful. It makes you see things that you don't usually pay attention to. Your inventory should include everything that belongs in your life. It should include people, things you do, habits, and things you don't do. You can even take a bigger step and include things you have.

Make a list of everything, and beside the ones that make you feel good, draw a happy face. If there are things or people on your list that didn't get a happy face, you know you need to remove them from your life. If that's not an option, because it is a family member or someone you work with, you should at least reduce the time you spend with them.

Think about everything you do. What is helping you and what is not? Who is helping you grow and who is holding you back?

Another inventory you can create is a **not-to-do list.** When you make yourself aware of the things you don't want to do, it makes it easier to prevent yourself from doing them.

Your list can look something like this:

I will not...

- Complain
- React
- Assume
- Take things personally
- Focus on things I don't want in my life
- Worry
- Overthink
- Judge
- Doubt (self)
- Be needy
- Make excuses
- Justify myself
- Repeat stories about problems
- Interrupt others when they are talking, even when I know or think I know what they are going to say
- Look at my phone first thing in the morning

Letting Go of Resentment

Another tool you can use to help you eliminate the extra baggage you have been carrying everywhere, is the resentment therapy. This one works to let go—not so much of people and things, but more of the emotional baggage you carry with you that you might not even realize.

Will the Real You Please Stand Up

This excess baggage could be the result of a situation that happened in the past, but not being aware of it holds you down. When you become aware of it, you can make peace and release it. You would be surprised at the things you will come up with.

I have seen it all, from a client being upset because another kid didn't let her play hide and seek when she was 8, to another being heartbroken after being told she was too skinny, by the boy she had a crush on in high school.

Make your list. Go all the way back to the earliest memory you have. I don't recommend spending too much time doing this. I don't want you to overload yourself with memories that could bring back negative emotions.

Limit yourself to doing a maximum of 5 minutes per day. I find that what works really well is to send love and forgiveness to them. At the end of each day, some clients burn their lists; others keep them in their journal.

There is no right or wrong; whatever feels good for you is the right way. No, I am not telling you to go contact anyone. Please avoid the urge of sending it to the person that has hurt you. They most likely don't even remember saying or doing anything.

This tool will help you release the emotions you have been holding onto, sometimes without even knowing it. It's all just memories, and sometimes they are not even the truth.

If you experience difficulty letting it go, remember that you are doing this for yourself, not others. Sometimes it helps to think that people do what they know how to do, and if they knew better, they would have done better. Some don't even realize that their actions and words actually hurt people. This is not a tool to assist you to tolerate what others do, but to help you release any pain or suffering that you felt because of someone else's actions.

Remember, your conclusion was made with your childlike mind or a past self, and you probably didn't have all the information to make a good judgement of the situation as you do now.

Chapter 6

When You Forget Who You Are

*"Accept. Then act.
Accept it as if you had chosen it.
Work with it, not against it.
Make it your friend."*
— Eckhart Tolle

Triggers Are Your Guides

My sons are my biggest teachers. I think all kids are. Whenever you get triggered, you are having an opportunity to see something you need to heal or learn from.

Triggers are your guide. We are always attracting people and experiences to help us heal. Every experience is a lesson, and people are just delivering it to you.

I have learned and always share with my clients that when triggered, to observe the situation and to avoid reacting to it. If you notice that you can't control your reaction at the moment, the best thing to do is to let the other people involved know that you want to talk to them about it but need some alone time first.

Sometimes walking away makes you realize that you don't even need to say anything else. Please don't just walk away without saying a word; that will not do any good either. It will make the other person feel abandoned and that you don't care.

Try saying something like, "I want to talk to you, but right now I feel that anything I say might not come out the way I actually feel. I need a few minutes to think and reflect so that I can release some emotions. I will be right back.

Like a mirror, your life is showing you reflections of what is within. Others are showing you areas of opportunities for you to improve and grow. That is the only reason you notice those things and feel the way you feel.

Your mind works like a filter, and when new experiences come up, it first goes to your memory storage and looks for a similar situation. Your mind wants to keep you safe, and it tries to prevent past pain from happening again, but that doesn't mean it will.

The people you are experiencing it with are nothing but messengers. When you get triggered next time, try to ask yourself where you have felt that emotion before. Is the same thing happening again, or was it just a trigger that brought back old memories?

Another scenario I will use as an example is when something happens in your relationship that makes you feel you are not important in the other person's life. Is that true, or is it just a reflection of how you treat yourself? If you are not making yourself a priority in your own life, how do you expect others to?

Stop Reacting, Start Living

Life is about how you react when everything seems to be going wrong. It's not what happens in your life that shapes your reality, but how you react to it. Learn to become transparent, and let others' energy and emotions pass right through you.

When you are always reacting, you are not being your true self, and it stops you from receiving all the goodies you have been expecting to receive.

What is your attitude toward life?

What is your attitude about your current situation?

If you can see and understand that there is always a positive in everything that happens to you, things will start manifesting for you.

It's as if life is testing you and wants you to prove that you want the things you want. You say you want certain things. You focus on the positive. You understand that your thoughts attract things. But how do you react when things are the opposite?

The tool you can use here is to reduce reaction. This is a very important part of life. How much importance do you give to the things you see?

Reaction goes with perspective. There are always different angles to look at every situation, and different angles will show you different views.

Different views will awaken different emotions. Different emotions will change how you react. Emotions create the lenses with which you see things. Emotions come from memories that you have stored in your mind.

The way you react to things is based on how your mind associates what you are now seeing with a past experience.

Different people will see the same situation differently because their reality and experiences are different. There is no right or wrong.

So if different people can have different reactions to the same situation, you can then flip the switch and change how you react to it, and by doing so, you can have a different outcome. Therefore, how you react to a situation will shape the outcome.

Reality is a mirror that reflects your attitude. You tend to get pushed off the tracks when something unexpected happens, but it doesn't have to be this way.

Your life will change when you realize that the problem is not life but you. You are the only one that can change your reality, and you start by taking full responsibility for your life. Until you start taking responsibility, life will keep reflecting your attitude, and guess what? I told you this before: If you think life is hard, it will be hard.

I want you to know this: Everything that is happening now is a manifestation of the past. You created this. If you want your life to change, you need to create new things.

You have been so used to blaming others for your current circumstances that it might take some effort to find some positive right now; but I promise you, if you look for it, you will find it.

Emotions are simply different degrees of the same thing, and knowing this gives you power to control how you react to things.

Don't get distracted by the small things. Always remind yourself of the picture-perfect vision you have created, and don't doubt it for a second. Every time you doubt, you stay stuck.

Don't Think; Feel

Your emotions are your guidance system, as well as the factor that attracts everything that shows up in your life. We all have the ability to tune in to our inner guidance.

Your mind is doing an amazing job trying to keep you safe; but unfortunately, it does sometimes prevent you from experiencing life and what you are here to live. It wants to keep you where it's familiar and comfortable.

Being emotional is natural, and knowing how to use your emotions to guide you makes life a lot easier to manoeuvre, and will lead you to what is intended to be yours.

Your emotions are the most important tool you have in life. Your mood creates your reality and controls your life.

Emotions are your body's reactions to the mind. Your mind is made of emotions, just like your body is made of atoms.

A lot of people grow up being told not to let their emotions show, and that having emotions means they are weak; and as a result, they hide their emotions. What a lot of people don't know is that suppressing your emotions can lead to sickness.

All a feeling wants is to be felt. You need to feel your feelings and learn to let them go.

Hiding them does not "fix" the problem, and life will keep presenting situations to help you release those suppressed emotions. Until you do so, you will keep experiencing repetitive emotional cycles.

If you are sad, accept that you are sad. Feel the feeling so that it can be released. By accepting what you feel, it allows you not to stay stuck. When you do that, you will notice that the feeling disappears.

Don't pretend to be happy when you are not. It's important to remember that you are not your emotions. Just feel it, observe it, acknowledge its presence, and let it go.

Will the Real You Please Stand Up

It's important not to identify yourself with the emotions you are feeling. There is no need to categorize it as bad or good; doing so gives it too much reality and could lead you into a blaming game, in search of reasons and someone to blame.

There is nothing to be fixed. A low emotion is not a problem to resolve. Even nature has its highs and lows. Everything has its tides. It's natural; you just have to learn to swing with it.

For me, I find that in low tides, self-care and naps are the best. Other days, I find that those are my best days—I get creative, and anything and everything becomes a font of inspiration for me.

Remember that when you are feeling any kind of emotional lows, not being in your true self-state, which is the positive state, you are going into old memories and issues of the past.

Your brain is putting labels on the present situation, and searching for past issues to match it. All it is doing is trying to keep you safe, but it's all an illusion.

Past memories were experienced by your old self, with the mind you had when it happened; but you grew, and they no longer serve you. Until you are ready to master your emotions, I strongly suggest that you create a self-care routine for the low tides.

Let your emotions guide you. Every morning, ask yourself, "How do I want to feel right now?"

What emotions do you want to feel daily?

How would you feel if your desires were already manifested?

Start by identifying 3–5 emotions that you want to feel every day, and make a list of things you can do that will help you feel those emotions.

There is no right or wrong here; whatever works for you is for you.

Think of the vibration and frequency of having what you want. Align yourself with the emotions of what you want to experience. Emotions are like waves that are always moving, and knowing how to ride them will be extremely beneficial to you.

I recommended keeping track of those emotions for a few days. I have noticed that there is usually a cycle, and knowing what your cycle is will help you identify what is coming next, and you can use it to your advantage.

Here is a list of some examples to help you create your own list:

- Do something spontaneous and exciting
- Watch a funny movie
- Spend time with friends
- Go for a walk
- Take a nap
- Meditate
- Listen to music
- Play with pets
- Journal
- Hug someone
- Deep breathing exercises
- Move your body
- Dance
- Create something new
- Take a personal development course
- Take a course in a new subject
- Clean up your clutter

It's important to make this list, and even more important than creating it is making time to do these things when you are feeling down. Make them a priority!

The low times can be the most transformative times. Melancholy is natural, and it can be the source of inspiration, like a muse is to an artist.

Multiple Layers of Reality

There are multiple angles of looking at everything, and it's all about the way you are looking at it. When an outsider looks at your life, he might have a completely different view about your life, depending on where he is looking from, and also depending on how he sees the world.

One circumstance can have lots of truths. Your perception is your reality. What happened to you shapes how you view the world, and it's the brain's job to scare you from doing something that could hurt you again.

The way we view the world is based on our limited experiences and beliefs, and sometimes we ignore and forget that other views can be equally true.

You have a choice. Everything is a choice. You choose what to focus on.

So please... Focus on what is working for you. And remember that there is always a positive to your negative. Life will always present you with both. It's up to you to choose which one you will focus on.

If you focus on the lack of something, lack is what you will get more of. Instead, find things to be grateful for.

Gratitude is extremely powerful, and when you focus on that, more shows up.

If you keep looking for things you dislike about yourself, you will keep attracting people to dislike them too.

You don't see things as they are; you see things as you are, and what's true for you might not be true for someone else.

Use positive eyes to transform your disappointments into success and positive outcomes. When you look at life from different angles, you are basically allowing a new remapping of your brain to take place. It allows you to take fear and change its meaning to something powerful.

When you get rid of a negative view by replacing it with a positive one, you are making room for the experience to completely transform.

Your mind is a tool, except you didn't get the instructions with it, so you need to figure out how it works. Your mind's job is to do what you tell it to do, and what it only knows how.

Keep in mind that what you are currently experiencing is a projection of your world within.

If the outside doesn't match what you desire, you are the only one that can change it by starting from within. Your perception is your reality.

Chapter 7

Money Has Ears and It Hears When You Call

"Money is usually attracted, not pursued."
– Jim Rohn

Find Your Own Version of Happiness

In this chapter, we are going to go deep and find your own version of happiness with money. Talking about money can be tricky, especially if you are experiencing a lack of it. Like any relationship, you have to work on it.

The secret about money is to treat it as a family member, someone you appreciate. People love people who appreciate them, and money is no different.

Happy people become wealthy faster because they are more appealing to others.

I was born in Brazil, and as in most Latin countries, you see people spending all their earnings to have a good time, and not having much left to show for their hard work, but they are happy.

After moving to Canada and growing up there, I experienced the opposite. Canada gives you the opportunity to be and have anything you want, but I find that most people are so focused on "having" that they forget to "be." They are so focused on all the possibilities that they forget to appreciate the moment.

I realized that the lack of balance was due to their mindset and beliefs. People that don't make a lot of money don't believe that they can make more, so they accept life as it is and make the most of it. On the other hand, the ones that live in a place where they have so many opportunities want to make sure they take them and do all they can to not miss them.

I didn't want to have a lack but also didn't want to spend my life working hard without enjoying it, so I committed myself to learning all I could to achieve a place that would be in between. I wanted to make enough money to live comfortably, to actually live without experiencing lack. I wanted to never have to say no again to my family because of lack.

Money fear is the biggest fear in life. So how do you release money fear? A tool that has worked for me multiple times in my life, and which I teach my clients, is to picture the worst-case scenario, as I mentioned in a previous chapter.

In Canada, we have a fantastic social system; medical care is covered, and in the worst-case scenario, I knew I would be okay. Maybe I wouldn't enjoy it, but I knew I wasn't going to die if I had no money.

Here is the thing: Most likely, you will never get to the worst-case scenario if you do your part; but by imagining it, you will lose your fear, knowing that in the end you won't die from being broke.

Remember: No Deposit, No Return

What is your contribution to the world?

Some people are so focused on wanting more that they forget to give. You can't expect to get something for nothing. It's not about expecting to get something in return when you do something. Most of the time, you don't even get anything from the same place you have given something to. It's a cycle, and it has to flow. Give more than you take. That's one of the money secrets I discovered. Always add more value than you take in cash value. By doing so, you will receive what you want, but everyone else around you will also have more.

By now you have created your goals, and you know what you want in your life. Now it's time for you to decide what you are offering in exchange for the money you intend to receive. Money is not the end goal but a tool to use on the way to it. If you are not making enough, it's because you are not serving enough.

I made a commitment to myself that for every dollar that comes in from the #catchuptoher program, I am going to donate 10% to help women that are going through the things that I have gone through myself.

Money loves energy. When you are living your best life, nourishing your body, moving energy, and staying healthy, it attracts wealth. This goes back to Chapter one, where I talk about creating life tabs and how one affects the other. You have to work on every part to make it whole, and your relationship with money is a big one.

Focusing on appreciation for the things you get when you use money is also a way to let money flow into your life. Money loves to be appreciated. You should show appreciation, not only when you receive it but also when you spend it. After all, when you use money, you are receiving a service or goods for it.

It has been proven that it's impossible to feel upset or worried when you are experiencing gratitude. When you feel grateful, your brain releases serotonin and dopamine, the two neurotransmitters responsible for feeling good. If you are worried about money, appreciate it instead.

I will include some money affirmations at the end of the chapter, which have helped me transform my relationship with money.

I find that money is one of the biggest blocks for my clients, and once they are able to heal their money wounds, money starts to flow easily and effortlessly into their lives.

Money wounds usually come from scripts that you have grown up listening to, and until now, you believed them. These beliefs could have originated from family stories, personal experiences, or things you have been taught.

Most of the time, when I do this work with my clients, I find that a lot of the beliefs come from them witnessing arguments about money. Money wounds are beliefs that were memorized by your mind.

In order for money to flow easily into your life, it has to circulate. If money is circulating, it means that you are living.

When you spend money, it means someone is receiving it. That someone will go and spend it somewhere else, and eventually it comes back to you.

We think of money and almost immediately feel fear. We feel dependent on it to survive, to eat, and have a roof over our heads. You need to understand that if you are afraid of money, it will run the other way. If you are operating from a place of need, lack, or desperation, money will go in the opposite direction. Remember, money wants to be loved and appreciated.

If you are in debt, you can use your power within to become friends with money again, but you can't just sit around and expect it to magically appear in your bank account. You still need to take action. You have to find the right balance and have the right mindset to take action.

How do you talk about money? For the last 11 years, I have raised my three, now teenage boys by myself. I remember in the past when I had financial problems; it was difficult to change my relationship with money. I didn't understand it.

In the first few years of being a single mom, I lost my home a couple of times for not having money to pay rent. I have lived in my car for a few days after getting evicted and being too embarrassed to ask for help, and my kids have missed school because even though I had food at home, I didn't have money to buy school lunches, and the school did not allow them to use the microwave to warm up leftovers. But did I die? No, and I am better than ever. I no longer have to ask money for permission to buy or do things.

Money is just energy, and you can attract it.

When I think back, I remember exactly when everything changed for me: I hit rock bottom, and I think it was in all areas of my life. I remember sitting on my living room floor, crying and thinking that I have had enough, and I refused to keep living that way. Somehow I was going to get myself out of the hole and never have to say no to my kids again because of lack. And the first thing I did was to change how I answered when they asked me for money or to buy something they really wanted.

If you are a mom, you know how many times a day kids ask for things, and my go-to answers were always, "I don't have money," "you don't need it," or "that's too expensive." When I understood the power of my words and started to change them, things started to change.

Instead of saying that you are broke, affirm that you just choose to spend your money on something else.

Instead of saying that you can't afford it, ask yourself how you can afford it. The money energy hears you, and it circulates back to you when you show appreciation for it.

Be thankful for bills; they are proof that you have received something—a service or a product.

You need to shift the current situation to the ideal. If you are stuck in the "I don't have" mode, you will experience more of the "I don't haves." When you feel that you are in lack of something, you will attract situations of lack and people in need.

Those answers that I refused to keep on using are the same things that created my own limiting beliefs about money. We all have them, regardless of how many digits we have in our bank accounts. In order to change your relationship with money, you need to reprogram your mind and recreate a new set of beliefs.

What I am trying to tell you is that I just want you to know that you will be okay, and you can change your life by changing how you see the world.

The desire you have to make more money or be financially independent is the same as the unknown magic that makes a seed grow into a plant. It's life wanting to express itself fully.

There is nothing wrong in wanting to be wealthy. There is more than enough for everyone. You can't experience life to the fullest without good food, well-made clothes, and a warm home to rest and heal.

Don't spend out of alignment. You don't need things; you desire them. To need something carries a low vibration. As moms, we tend to tell our kids that they don't need the things they are asking for, when we can't or don't want to spend money getting them, and that teaches their subconscious that when they want something, they don't need it, even though it's what they desire.

If you want to experience riches, you can't think in poverty. The best you can do for everyone around you is to make the most of yourself.

You can't help others by not becoming better, by not having more.

I have heard so many people say that they want to be rich, but they are terrified to walk into a fancy store or go to a 5-star restaurant. How can you be wealthy if you don't feel that you are enough?

You have to show up as the person that can go into a fancy store and buy a 2000-dollar purse, if you want to be that person. Don't act as if you shouldn't be there, as if you were apologizing for it. You have to allow yourself to be "her"—the one that is not afraid—and to be open to receiving the best. Walk in the store as if you own it, not as someone that works there. Be confident.

Go on; go into the store as if you had all the money to buy whatever you wanted to. Try things on. Walk and talk like the person you want to be. Go take a tour at open houses that resemble your dream home. Test-drive your dream car.

Be Grateful for Your Bills

Most of my clients struggle with money. When I first start working with clients, I ask them how much money they need to make to live the life they want, and how much is enough.

The answer is almost the same most of the time: "As long as I have enough to pay my bills, I am good." Is that really enough? I want you to really think about that. If that is all you need, how is your life going to change really?

I am sure that one way or another, you have figured out ways to pay your bills. You might have been late a few times, or maybe a lot of times, but you always found a way. Unless you are homeless right now, on the streets, and starving, you have enough. That's what enough means—enough to survive.

I want you to think bigger than that. That's the only way that life is going to change for you and all others around you.

Stop being afraid of money; make money your friend. To help my clients work on their relationship with money, I share with them the technique for being grateful for bills. I want you to try it too.

Grab all your current bills. I want you to write across them: Thank you for the money to pay for services I have received. I also want you to grab a few bills you have already paid and, at the top, I want you to write: Thank you, paid. You can even add a happy face beside it if you want.

Be grateful for your bills. Your bills are proof that you have received services or products. Be grateful for your electricity bill; think of how you were able to do things at home because you had electricity. How about the internet? Aren't you grateful for being able to instantly connect to people in a totally different part of the globe? It has definitely made life so much easier.

Services were provided before you even paid for them, and that alone is a huge reason to be grateful for your bills.

When you are about to complain about money, ask yourself, "Do I want to push money away further?" Complaining stops the flow of money.

Money Affirmations

- I have money to share and spare.
- Money flows to me easily and effortlessly from expected and unexpected sources.
- Every time I spend money, money comes back to me multiplied.
- Wealth constantly flows into my life.

- My actions create constant prosperity.
- I am aligned with the energy of abundance.
- I deserve to make more money.
- The more money I make, the more I contribute.
- I have more than enough money.
- My life is filled with wealth and health.
- I am always discovering new sources of income.
- I am open to receive all the wealth life brings me.
- I am getting out of my way when it comes to money.
- I accept and receive unexpected money and prosperity.
- Today I commit to living my financial dreams.

Chapter 8

Receiving is the Twin Sister of Asking

*"We are Divine enough to ask
and we are important enough to receive."*
– Wayne Dyer

Be Open to Receive

Everyone deserves to have a fantastic, abundant life. You are good and worthy to receive abundance. Be open to receive, and allow all the good things in life to flow to you—all the food you want; great friends to have fun with; respect from others; and of course, receiving compliments.

Think back about all the things you have received in life, and be grateful for them; this opens the path to receive more of them. Claim it! Say it out loud: "I am open to receive more good things in my life!"

When you see yourself living in an abundant life, you are seeing one reality. When you see thousands of people living in abundance, the effect is a lot stronger, because it's causing a bigger impact.

You become successful by helping others become successful. You have to give what you want to receive. What you wish for another, you wish for yourself. The cycle starts with you. You first have to be the source of what you wish to experience in your own life.

Most of my coaching clients struggle with this part, and most people do, because they don't understand it. Therefore, they don't know how to do it. No one taught them how to receive.

You need to work on your capacity to receive.

Will the Real You Please Stand Up

When was the last time you let someone pay for your bill?

How about a gift? When was the last time you let someone buy you something?

How about taking a compliment? I have seen it all. You are so used to countering compliments with faults, that you don't even realize it. Can you accept a compliment with a simple "thank you," without deflecting it or making yourself small? There is no need to justify or explain; just say thank you! That's it!

If you can identify with the examples I just gave you, I bet that you have also dismissed other people that were thanking you, with a comment like: "No need to thank me; it was nothing." What do you mean, it was nothing? It was something! You did something for someone, so let them thank you for it!

Stop being shy about receiving; you are not doing anyone a favor by being that way. Think about the other way around, as if you were the giver. Would you feel rejected? It's a cycle. "Thanks, I accept that," should be the words coming out of your mouth. Do it for the giver! By allowing yourself to receive, you allow the giver the happiness of giving.

You need to unlearn what you have learned! There are mainly two reasons why you have been acting this way. You don't feel safe, or you don't think you are worthy, and unless you are at risk of experiencing physical harm, your fears are not real.

They are coming from your mind. Your mind is just a passenger in the vehicle, and it thinks it knows best. It tries to control your life by making up stories, but its only interest is to feel safe.

Receiving comes with the feminine energy; by not doing so, you are only blocking yourself from getting all the goodies you have been asking for.

Most people were never taught how to receive. They are so good at giving but struggle with the receiving part. Everything in the Universe runs in cycles, and by not being open to receiving, you are not letting the energy flow. The Universe is listening.

You don't need to feel guilty; there is plenty to go around!

This also works when you want things. Give that which you want to receive:

- Want approval, show approval.
- Want respect, show respect.
- Want to be loved, be loveable.

Instead of complaining to the world, love it instead.

Chapter 9

Elle et Lui

"The union of feminine and masculine energies within the individual is the basis of all creation."
– Shakti Gawain

Masculine and Feminine Energies

Everyone has masculine and feminine energies. This is part of the duality that makes everything in our world. Everything comes in pairs. These energies can be used as tools. Different things will require different energies.

Each energy has its own strengths and weaknesses, and in order to feel balanced and in harmony, we need both.

Understanding how they express and how one compliments the other will help you form a balanced union.

Both masculine and feminine energies have unhealthy and healthy aspects. When you become aware of how you use them, you can stop recreating the unhealthy patterns.

When they are not balanced, you look for things and people to complete you. When they are in balance, you are whole. You are complete as you are. You stop being a "half."

In relationships, if those energies are not balanced, it will create conflict with the other person's energy. When you take action from those unbalanced energies, you will likely attract another incomplete person, and that's the root for most unhealthy and toxic relationships. When you are complete in a relationship, you are happy and loving, not clingy and needy.

In relationships, the more opposed the energy between two beings, the stronger the attraction will be.

Stop and think of what is happening around you. See where you are going in too much or too little. Worrying about fitting in and being accepted blocks you from embracing your natural powers.

I want you to understand that these energies have nothing to do with gender, and it would be beneficial if both men and women would learn how to use both energies.

Society causes us to repress opposite gender traits; but to be whole, we need to integrate both. Single moms are a perfect example of mostly using masculine energy.

This was a big "aha" moment for me, as I have raised my kids for the past 11 years as a single mom. I was a masculine-based woman until I realized I was out of alignment. I had to be the nurturer but also the provider, and that's fine, but there has to be a balance between the two energies in order for the enchantress energy to come through. Sometimes it means putting one on hold to nurture the other.

Have you been operating in survival mode, using masculine energy all the time? If you answered yes, then you now know that you need to spend some time nurturing and loving your feminine side a little more.

Expressing your feelings is also a way to keep your energies balanced. When they are balanced, they reset.

Everything in life has both energies. Find ways to balance masculine and feminine energy. Too much of either can lower your vibration frequency. The secret is to find the perfect alchemy between the two.

Feminine energy is the Enchantress of life. This power comes from within once you realize how perfect you are. It taps into intuition and is connected to the unknown.

This energy is all about emotions and feelings and letting them be the guides.

It is expressive and non-judgemental.

It is gentle and nurturing.

When your feminine energy is balanced, you are confident, loveable, and open to receive love and to be pursued and led.

This is the energy that makes you have multiple projects at the same time, always looking for things to do. This is the energy that basically created the famous to-do lists.

When using this energy, you know you don't need to try; all you need to do is to focus on the energy of being.

If your feminine energy is imbalanced, you become over-giving, unable to accept change, overly emotional, needy, lacking in confidence, and jealous, and you feel unworthy. When a woman is in her feminine energy, there is no lack or neediness.

The sacred masculine energy is about courage, strength, clarity, focus, determination, and willpower. You use this energy when taking action. It uses logic and plans things, always with a sense of direction. It's protective and likes to lead; it doesn't care what others think; it initiates and is disciplined; it's brave and always takes charge; it's single-task oriented, loves a challenge, and is a problem solver. The sacred masculine energy wants freedom but also wants to be needed and respected.

When your masculine energy is not balanced, you experience conflicts and the need to control things. You are pushy, cold hearted, have low self-esteem, and lack confidence. You become confused and afraid to take action. Fear does that to the sacred masculine energy.

When both energies are balanced, they work together. You take action and initiate things with the masculine energy, using the feminine energy that intuitively knows the way and guides you. You take action to protect and provide for your family, knowing that even if it doesn't feel like it at the moment, everything will be okay. You take action in your business and, without pressure, you know you will be compensated for your effort and value provided. You give, knowing and accepting that you will receive. You don't need to force things into happening, because you know that what is for you, is coming to you. You are the point of attraction. You do the work and life delivers.

Are You Using Too Much Masculine Energy?

Being in the masculine energy all the time stops you from receiving. Money is masculine, and most of my clients that struggle with money have masculine wounds that need to be healed. It's time to come back to your feminine power. Release "Miss Independent," and reconnect with your Enchantress. Are you experiencing financial lack? This could easily be one of the reasons.

The same applies to your relationships—having unbalanced energies have a huge impact on what type of relationship you have. Going too much into masculine energy attracts men with too much feminine energy, and since that's not their energy, these men are needy and have low masculine power to meet the needs of a woman.

In the next chapter, I will share tips on how to increase and heal your feminine energy through self-care.

Chapter 10

SELF

*"Know, first, who you are,
and then adorn yourself accordingly."*
– Epictetus

www.willtherealyou.com

What is Self?

Self is everything you are that others are not. It's your identity. I believe that your purpose here is to learn and to remember who you are, but most importantly, you are here to love, to be loveable, and to be loved.

You are here to collect all the clues life gives you, and to put them together to complete a whole—the real you. The real you is love.

When you love yourself, you discover who you can become, who you want to become, and who you are afraid of becoming. When you combine all your discoveries, you get the master key that unlocks all the possibilities, which only the real you gets to experience.

Learn to relax when you get things done. Even better, celebrate it! When you celebrate, you express gratitude.

Take time for yourself; do nothing, or do something you really enjoy doing. Spend time with friends or go to the beach. Whatever makes you happy, do it!

Do yoga or dancing; move your body, move your energy. Moving your body helps you reset and balance your energies.

Will the Real You Please Stand Up

Self-care is so important. Self-care is self-love. How can you show love for yourself today? How can you help someone else today? Nurture yourself and others today. How about some hugs? Everybody loves to be loved, not just kids.

Be vulnerable and give yourself the opportunity to experience new things.

Stop being a people pleaser. Learn to say no when you want to say no.

Wear looser clothes—dresses, or maybe something floral? How about doing a 30-day, no-pants challenge?

Set boundaries; what are you tolerating? What you tolerate is what you allow to be in your life.

Get creative. Start something new. When was the last time you did something for the first time? I used to tell myself that I wasn't creative, until I learned that it was a limiting belief that I had. Because of it, years went by without me trying to do new things. Now I know that creativity gets better as I use it.

Rearrange your room. Not only will you be using your creativity by doing it, but you will also be cleaning the energy. You can use that time to declutter too.

Do arts and crafts with your kids. How about getting yourself a coloring book for adults? I was amazed when I found out such a thing exists. Some of them are actually really funny. This is perfect for inner child healing, and for increasing your feminine energy.

Meditation is powerful, and a great tool. When your thinking mind is still, then you see reality. If you are like most people, when you close your eyes and sit in silence, it's a big mess inside your head. Thoughts are racing through from every possible direction, rambling on about everything and anything.

The key is to observe them, without attaching any feeling or judgement to them, and let them pass by. Different people have different ways of meditating. Whatever works for you is the right way for you. If meditation, for you, is when you go for a walk, then that works too.

Self-Discovery:
Powerful Questions to Help You Know Yourself

Questions have power—lots of power. Grab your journal and ask yourself questions. You don't need to do them all at once. Don't force yourself to answer them; 2–3 times a week should do it.

I don't want you to just ask yourself questions that you already know the answers to, like your favorite colors or food. I want you to go deep into your thoughts and beliefs. This will help you see which ones are actually yours and which ones were given to you when you were growing up.

By getting to know yourself really, really well, it will be easier to live on purpose with a purpose. You have to be willing to be vulnerable and honest with your answers in order to really know yourself. If you are scared that someone will see your answers, you can write them on a piece of paper instead, and get rid of it after each session you have with yourself.

So, where do you start, and what questions should you ask? Here are some questions you can start with.

- What would be the most exciting thing for you to do right now?

- What can you do today to connect with the version of yourself you intend to become?
- What is something you love doing, even when you are tired or rushed?
- What can you do today that you have never done?
- What is the message your subconscious is trying to send you? (feeling)
- Is what you are doing helping you with your goal?
- What limiting beliefs are you responding to?
- Will the problem that you are worried about now, be important in the future?
- If so, is there anything you can do about it?
- How can you be better?
- Whom can you help today?
- How can you resolve this issue?
- How can you earn more money?
- Are you using "being busy" as an excuse, out of fear, to not do the things you know you should be doing?
- If a relationship or job makes you unhappy, do you choose to stay or leave?
- Are the thoughts you are thinking about, what you want to create in your life?
- How are you really? Are you finding yourself or creating yourself?
- When was the last time you invested in yourself?
- Who do you desire to be in the world?
- When was the last time you did something for the first time?
- Think of someone you admire. What does she/he do?
- What are you avoiding and why?
- What would you do if you knew you couldn't fail?
- Are you better today than you were yesterday?
- If you could have one single wish granted today, what would it be?
- Is the life that you are living, the life you want to be living?
- What would you do with your life if you knew there were no limits?
- When was the last time you told yourself, "I love you?"

- How would you act if you were the best in the world at what you do?
- Are your actions guided by love or fear?
- Do the people around you add value to your life?
- Are you a human *being* or a human *doing*?
- When was the last time you made a new friend?
- Are you holding onto something you need to let go of?
- What would you do differently if you knew nobody would judge you?
- Whom do you admire the most in the world?
- Are you uncomfortable talking to people you don't know?
- When was the last time you did something for fun?
- What could you do today to improve your life?
- When was the last time you told yourself, "I am enough?"
- Are you a pleasant person to be around?
- What is your heart telling you that you are not listening to?
- When do you feel the most confident?
- How do you recharge?
- Are you comfortable being uncomfortable?
- Can you be alone without feeling lonely?
- How do you feel about your parents?
- What does your ideal life look like?
- What does your ideal day look like?
- What does your ideal self look like?
- What does it take for you to feel loved?
- What do you think about most often?
- Do you enjoy your own company?
- Who is the most important person in your life?
- What is the one thing you love the most about yourself?
- What was the greatest day of your life?
- What is your biggest self-limiting belief?
- What role does gratitude play in your life?
- What memories instantly make you smile?
- Do you take things personally?
- Have you ever felt truly loved by yourself?

Will the Real You Please Stand Up

- How do you feel about growing old someday?
- What lies do you tell yourself (such as, "I am not enough," or "no one will ever love me")?
- Have you ever felt loved by someone else? If so, can you remember a moment where you were filled with love?
- Who are the people that believe in you?
- What do you want to be remembered for?
- What makes you happy?
- If you could live anywhere in the world, where would you live?
- What are you most thankful for?
- How many hours a week would the ideal workweek have?
- What are you looking for in a relationship?
- What does family mean to you?
- How is your relationship with money?
- What is holding you back from living the life you want?
- What are 5 things that can put a smile on your face no matter what?
- If you found out that you inherited 1 million dollars from an aunt you had never even heard of, how would you spend that money?
- What if you find out that you could get that money 1 year from now?
- What would be your plans?
- Do you believe in a greater force (religiously or simply the power of the Universe)?
- Is there something inside of you that is blocking love from your life (maybe a limiting belief or past hurt)?
- What is your happiest memory?
- If you could have any career, what would it be?
- What are your superpowers?
- What is your greatest fear? Is it real?
- What matters the most in your life?
- Do you prefer to spend time alone or with people?
- Do you feel that you know your purpose in life?
- If you could go back 10 years, what would you change?

www.willtherealyou.com

- What are two emotions you would like to feel every day?
- What do you believe is the meaning of life?

There... I hope this helps...

Chapter 11

When You Meet You

*"The more you praise and celebrate your life,
the more there is in life to celebrate. "*
– **Oprah Winfrey**

Gratitude

Gratitude is one of the most powerful tools in life. When you are in a state of gratitude, more things that you are grateful for will show up.

Appreciate the small things. When was the last time you stopped to watch the raindrops? We are so busy living the so-called life that we take those things for granted. Most people hardly ever stop to count their blessings, and tend to fall into negative thinking, complaining about traffic, people, their finances, etc. They get addicted to that thinking pattern where even when they don't have anything to complain about, they go looking for things.

Start you day listing things you are grateful for and watch your life transform.

Secrets of Life

- You don't have to be good at everything.
- If you are waiting to be ready to start, you are starting too late.
- What is true for you, might not be for someone else.
- Everyone has a different truth.
- People don't notice your mistakes as much as you think.
- Treat everyone as an old friend.
- Always gift people when you see them, with a thought, a gift, or a blessing.

Will the Real You Please Stand Up

- Give away what you haven't touched in the last 12 months.
- Remember: no deposit, no return.
- Act the way in which the person you want to be would act.
- There is only now.
- Love is always the answer.
- A setback is a disguised setup.
- The Universe doesn't speak any language; it speaks frequency.
- Every time you make a decision, you shift.
- Learn how to swing the ups and downs; there is nothing to fix.
- Be interested, not interesting.
- Follow the 5-minute rule: If it takes less than 5 minutes, do it now.
- Other people see the world with different eyes.
- Instead of making assumptions, ask.
- Be present when you are doing the things you love.
- The past is gone. Let it go. There is nothing you can do.
- Be impeccable with your words.
- Words have power.
- Don't try to change others; you can only change yourself.
- Quit nagging.
- Remove expectations.
- Take full responsibility for your life.
- Don't blame anyone for your outcomes.
- Hang out with friends you would want your children to have.
- Remember, if people knew better, they would do better.
- Stretching removes blocks and stuck energy.
- Pain is usually related to self-love and limiting beliefs.
- Your health is a response to how you treat yourself.
- Eating well is a form of self-respect.
- Illness is created when you aren't loving yourself enough, and it comes to release old energies.
- Organize and minimize; your physical surrounding influences how you feel.
- Do it for yourself; your future self will love you for it.
- Aim higher; possibilities are limitless.

- Journal; everything you need is already inside of you—let it come out.
- Make play a priority.
- Do the unexpected.
- Remember birthdays.
- Connect to 3 people daily (old friends or make new ones).
- Feel good first; then do it.
- All you need is an intention or a decision. That's it!

Celebration

Have you stopped to wonder what it will feel like when you finally meet *you*? You know the feeling you get when you think you found the one? You feel a surge of happiness, and everything just seems to move so easily and effortlessly.

When you finally meet *you*—the real you—everything else in life just flows. You understand how you see the world and all the layers. It becomes easy just being. You feel calm, at peace, and genuinely happy.

I remember the day when I finally loved myself enough to say "I love me." It was a normal weekday. I remember the feeling as if it were this morning. I remember opening my eyes and just smiling. I was literally smiling for no apparent reason. I was filled with overwhelming excitement. I wanted to jump out of bed and dance. I even questioned myself why I was so happy. That's when I realized that I was happy because I felt at home, totally comfortable, and able to be myself. I was done with the struggles and was willing to surrender.

This is the moment I have been waiting for, the reason that I wrote this book. I wanted you to experience the magic of being your true self. I wanted everyone to have what I wanted for myself. I am confident that if you do the work and are reading what I am writing, you will know exactly what I mean.

Will the Real You Please Stand Up

You now have the key that fits all the locks, and the tools to use to light the spark as you go. You feel safe enough to open all the locks. You feel like your truest self came out, and you can be who you are meant to be. It sounds romantic. It is.

You stop looking for the perfect one to complete you because you are complete. When you get involved in a love relationship, it feels right because you are already happy, and you attract people that are the same way.

You understand that you are not perfect; you are human, with flaws, weaknesses, and history. But those flaws don't define you. You are much more than that.

It's incredibly special when you believe in yourself. I would say it's almost the same or even better than the feeling you get when you feel like you have found your soulmate. You feel complete.

When you finally catch up to her, you feel more courageous, more accepting of who you are, and more willing to take risks. Everything just flows. There is a feeling of experiencing more in life. You feel like the pieces are finally clicking together.

Life is still the same, even though it feels like you created a new life. The reality is that all the work you have done changed your perspective about life. And that is the magic of being you. There is beauty all around you, and now you can see it too.

If you still need me to point out and tell you exactly what you are feeling right now, here it is:

- You are now comfortable being your most authentic self.
- Your goals and values are aligned with your purpose.
- You start seeing different layers of the world around you that you have never seen before, and it's just beautiful.

- You attract amazing people into your life and business.
- You become an observer and know how to handle the super highs, the down lows, and everything in between. You know how to ride the waves.
- You share your story with others, and it inspires them.
- You feel energetic and alive.
- You feel incredibly lucky; you feel blessed.
- You are filled with gratitude.
- You are more intuitive, and understand that it's not your mind that guides you but your feelings. You trust your gut.
- You never ever settle; you know your worth.
- You understand that you can't get it wrong, because you are never done growing. There is always a next-level self.
- You feel happy in a way that you can only remember feeling as a child, and the whole world seems like the magical place it was back then too.
- You feel a happy kind of nervousness. When nerves and joy coincide, you get butterflies!
- You are open to receive all the goodies life has to offer.
- You feel ridiculously inspired. You are more creative with your work, and find that ideas keep coming in.
- You feel more connected to everything and everyone. A feeling of "we are all one" vibrates inside of you.

It's as if an unknown weight has been lifted from your shoulders. Life doesn't seem hard anymore, and you know that you have all the power and guidance you need inside of you.

You are now invited! It's time to celebrate!

Don't make it a one-time thing. Every day is the perfect day to do it. Every chance you get, take it. You now have so many reasons why. So make it count. Make the party last forever. Celebrate you and all you do.

Will the Real You Please Stand Up

The Start

www.willtherealyou.com

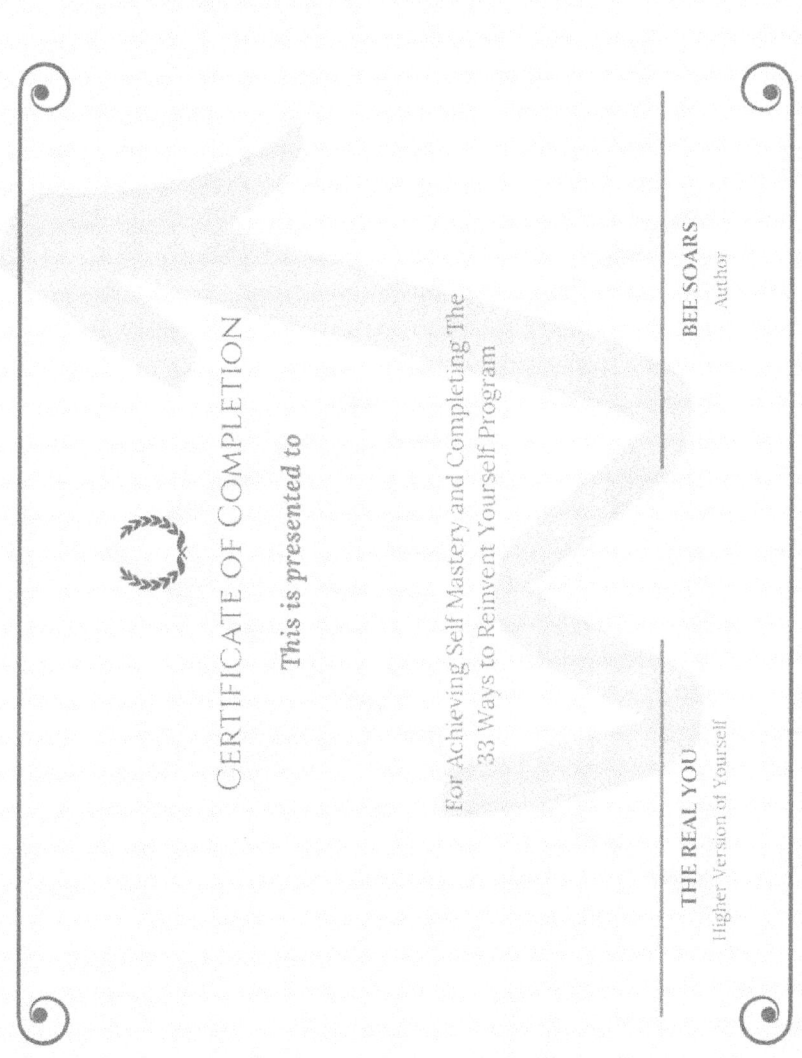

About the Author

Bee Soars is a mother of three sons who are growing into manhood. As a child she had a beautiful loving upbringing, and as a teen she moved to Canada from Brazil with her family.

She experienced a deep spiritual awakening when one of her sons was diagnosed with childhood Leukemia at age 2.

As a single mother with three boys after a failed 10-year relationship, she tried to recreate a perfect family but found herself walking on egg shells, married to an unstable schizophrenic man.

Bee didn't know what was in her until she had to bring it out. Her natural resilience led her to a remarkable ability to start over and reinvent herself after experiencing heartaches and hitting rock bottom multiple times.

Bee began to study psychology and ancient forms of spirituality, and later went on to become a NeuroLinguistic Programming Coach and Practitioner and a Spiritual and Life Purpose Coach, among other certifications and trainings.

Bee's teachings and techniques have already helped countless people around the world to reinvent themselves and awaken their inner essence to reclaim their power and recreate their lives from within.

She knows all about resetting yourself in order to love, live, parent and lead.

www.ingramcontent.com/pod-product-compliance
Lightning Source LLC
Chambersburg PA
CBHW062224080426
42734CB00010B/2021